THE INSTITUTE OF POLITICS PUBLICATIONS
WILLIAMS COLLEGE, WILLIAMSTOWN, MASS.

THE PREVENTION OF WAR

OTHER INSTITUTE OF POLITICS PUBLICATIONS ISSUED BY THE YALE UNIVERSITY PRESS

ROUND-TABLE CONFERENCES OF THE INSTITUTE OF POLITICS AT ITS FIRST SESSION 1921

THE RECENT AIMS AND POLITICAL DEVELOPMENT OF JAPAN. BY RIKITARO FUJISAWA, Ph.D.

THE PREVENTION OF WAR

BY

PHILIP KERR AND LIONEL CURTIS

NEW HAVEN
PUBLISHED FOR THE INSTITUTE OF POLITICS
BY THE YALE UNIVERSITY PRESS

NEW HAVEN · YALE UNIVERSITY PRESS
LONDON · HUMPHREY MILFORD · OXFORD UNIVERSITY PRESS

MCMXXIII

Printed in the United States of America

PREFACE

The lectures in this volume were delivered at the Institute of Politics at Williamstown by two British authors, under the general title, "A British View of International Problems." They are now published under what is a more appropriate title, "The Prevention of War," because the first three deal specifically with the problem of ending international war, and because the other three deal with special aspects of the same problem. The lecture on "The Union of South Africa" describes the causes which gave rise to the South African war (1899-1902) and how they were finally removed. The lecture on "Responsible Government in India" sets forth the attempt which is being made in that vast country to effect the transition from benevolent despotism to self-government without the anarchy or civil war which has almost always accompanied that transition in the past. The third lecture discusses the relations between Europe and Asia, and the place of moral ideas in the progress of mankind to lasting liberty and peace.

CONTENTS

LECTURE | | PAGE

I The Mechanical Reason for War . . 7

II The Psychological Reason for War . 29

III The Only Road to International Peace 49

BY PHILIP KERR

I The Union of South Africa 77

II Responsible Government in India . . 107

III A Criterion of Values in International Affairs 135

BY LIONEL CURTIS

Index 163

BY
PHILIP KERR

THE PREVENTION OF WAR

LECTURE I

The Mechanical Reason for War

I propose to take war and the possibility of preventing it as the subject of these lectures, partly because nobody can escape the responsibility of doing what he can to prevent a repetition of the events of the past eight years, and partly because war is an essential element in international relations. In every other sphere of human relations, laws conceived according to the dictates of reason, justice and humanity can be invoked to settle disputes, and the appeal to violence is not only forbidden, but is treated as a crime. In international relations force is the only court of appeal, the only means of redress. There is no international legislature to define the law, no adequate court to interpret the law, no policeman to enforce obedience to the law. If diplomacy, which is simply another name for negotiations, fails, there are no alternatives between submission to what both parties probably regard as an injustice, and unleashing the savage hounds of war. Nobody can take a single step in the study of international affairs without being brought up against the question of war.

What I have to say may be of some interest to you because not only have I been a student of international politics for many years, but from the end of 1916 till a year ago I was almost as close to the center of world affairs as it was possible for a man to be. There was no secret of the British government that I did not know, no paper that I did not or could not read, hardly any conference that I could not attend. I have witnessed from the inside the gigantic efforts made to win the war, and the hardly less gigantic efforts made to save the peace. What I have to say, therefore, is based upon some real knowledge of the way in which the affairs of nations are conducted, and is not, though at times it may seem to be, merely academic.

The question I have been asking myself for the last two or three years has been this: Have we, as the result of the terrible experiences of the late war, and of the victory of the Allies, any real security against a repetition of a world war? To this question I have to answer, No.

For the moment we have peace in the military sense, and there is no danger of a war such as that of 1914, because Germany is disarmed and the preponderance of military strength on the allied side is simply overwhelming. Further, I do not believe that the peoples who fought in the last war would submit to be driven to such wholesale slaughter again. They are, I believe, substantially immune from the kind of militarism which drove them to death by the million in 1914. The menace today is anarchy and economic chaos, involving local fighting about frontiers, with Europe retreating towards barbarism, as the habits of order, and the machinery of production and exchange, break down. These dangers are very real and are being discussed in the Round Tables. I believe that in time they will be overcome, for reason and common sense will eventually make headway against passion, ignorance and fear. In any case I do not propose to discuss them. What I want to do is to consider what are the fundamental underlying causes of world wars. For until we understand these and deal with them, all the industry and zeal and good-will spent in repairing the damage wrought by the late war, and in restoring normal conditions, will not prevent such a war from breaking out again.

If we look back through history we shall see that what has happened in the last eight years is not a unique or isolated phenomenon. There was a world war for the first fifteen years of the last century, ending with the battle of Waterloo. Like the late war, it swept away some great abuses—for instance, European feudalism—and paved the way for better things. Before that, again, there was the world war which centered in the long struggle for the control of the New World and ended in 1763. There was the world war which was concluded by the Treaty of Utrecht in 1713, which recorded the failure of Louis XIV to establish an ascendancy over Europe. There was the Thirty Years' War, ended by the Treaty of Westphalia in 1648, during which the population of Germany is said to have fallen from thirty millions to eight millions. And so we can trace back through the ages a steady procession of devastating wars, engulfing the whole of the then civilized world, followed by peaces of exhaustion, which in turn give way to new eras of war.

Have we really any reason for thinking that wars are any less likely in the future than they have been in the past? An American historian, John Fiske, writing in 1894, declared that "since 1815, the civilized world has been more successful than ever before in keeping clear of war. It is close upon eighty years since 1815, and in this time Europe has seen about ten years of war, and the United States about six years; but in the eighty years before 1815 Europe saw about fifty years of war, and the United States as many as twenty years." Fiske wrote these confident words just before the Spanish-American War, the Chino-Japanese War, the Boer War, the Russo-Japanese War, the Balkan Wars, the Italo-Turkish War, and the Great War—twenty-five years of almost uninterrupted war.

Moreover, at the end of each of these eras of war, men, as in 1918, turned feebly to the creation of some machinery which would prevent the repetition of the catastrophe. In 1713 the Abbé de St. Pierre published "A Project of a Treaty for Perpetual Peace," which exercised much influence on the minds of statesmen at that time. In 1795 Immanuel Kant, the great philosopher, published his treatise "On Perpetual Peace," in which he proposed that the law of nations should be established by a federation of free states. A few years later, before he became intoxicated with imperial dreams, Napoleon thought of concentrating the great European peoples into a confederation with a central assembly modelled on the American Congress or the Amphictyonic Assembly of Greece to watch over the common weal "of the great European family." In 1814 the Emperor Alexander II of Russia, anticipating the disarmament project of his successor discussed at The Hague nearly a century later, came to Paris filled with the dream of uniting Europe in a League of Peace. Then, as now, men's mouths were filled with talk about preventing war. A League of Peace was actually created, and in the concert of Europe and the Holy Alliance, Europe had a piece of machinery which did prevent war for a generation. But as you all know, it gradually became an engine for reaction. England drew aloof. The promulgation of the Monroe Doctrine excluded the New World from its scope. The revolutionary movements of 1848 destroyed its waning power, and within a few years there followed the Crimean War, and the three wars which Bismarck waged to create modern Germany, and there began that era of competitive armaments which ended in the cataclysm of 1914.

When the next world war does come, what will it be like? As the last war shows, when the national existence is at stake every international rule for making war less horrible is ruthlessly swept aside. Some nation will enlist every latest discovery of natural science in order that it may save itself, and then every other belligerent will do the same in self-defense. It is the wildest folly to imagine anything else. You cannot humanize war. You can only abolish it. So if mankind goes to sleep again, as it has done so often in the past, it will awake to find itself engaged in military operations, the basis of which will be the use of poison gas, aeroplanes dropping explosives and gas bombs far and wide over defenseless cities, submarines, and all the horrible refinements that radioactivity and other similar developments will introduce into the conduct of war. And just because every year modern invention shrinks the world, and every people becomes more involved with every other, in trade, in finance, in knowledge, in politics, the occasions of international dispute are rapidly multiplying, and every local war will tend all the more rapidly to become a world war. You can see the process in the contrast between the proportion of humanity engaged and the part played by the United States, in the world war which raged in 1812 and that which ended in 1918.

You may think that these remarks indicate pessimism. They are uttered in a spirit exactly the reverse. I believe that public opinion, the world over, has never been so opposed to war as a method of settling international disputes as it is today, has never been so anxious to find a way of preventing it, and has never been in a stronger position for giving effect to its desires. The real danger today is that people, appalled by the apparent complexity of the problem, led astray by a vague and wordy idealism which does not think the problem out to the bottom, and preoccupied by their own affairs, will drift on during the era of comparative peace which is now due, only to wake up to find themselves plunged in war again. This is exactly what happened to Great Britain in 1914. Despite the constant warnings of well-known writers and statesmen, it was not until after the German invasion of Belgium, and the General Staff frightfulness there, that the general public realized what was going on, and that it had no option but to go through with the war. And it was still more true of the United States. No nation thought less of war. No nation was more anxious to help to make peace. Yet gradually she found that she was faced with the inexorable necessity of going to war, because she had been asleep so far as the outside world was concerned, and there was no other way in which she could save freedom. I am not afraid of another world war if the leading nations really give consistent and constructive thought to the problem of how it may be prevented.

Mr. Curtis, in his last lecture, has pointed out that liberty rather than peace is the true goal of human activity; and that he who seeks peace merely to save his life will never find it. There is profound truth in these statements. War is not the worst thing in the world, as you can see from your own Civil War, and as half mankind was driven to see in the Great War. Progress is the law of life, and sometimes, when the barriers of reaction or the forces of oppression are very unyielding, liberty has had to arm itself with the sword.

But the question I wish to discuss today is this: Is war really necessary to human progress? Must we continue to submit to a regular recurrence of these appalling evils every few decades as the price of winning more freedom for humanity? Is war, so to speak, a law of nature? Or is it, like duelling, or ordeal by fire, or stage coaches, or sailing vessels, an expedient, natural, perhaps, in a primitive age, but one which can be superseded by something better as common sense and clear thinking and good will are brought to bear upon the problem?

I would answer unhesitatingly that war is barbarism, that it is not inevitable, and that if it takes place between civilized powers, it is because they have failed to create an alternative system whereby their disputes, or the great issues involved in human progress, can be settled by other and more sensible means.

The causes of war are legion. There have been wars of conquest, of religion, of race, of nationality, of liberation, in the past. There are wars of race and nationality and color, and of trade and commerce, looming up in the future. Can anybody who surveys the world today, with Africa just stirring into life, with Asia once more on the move, with Russia Bolshevized, with the Mohammedans beginning to unite, with the all-pervading question of the color line, with half the nations of Europe profoundly aggrieved by the results of the war—can anyone believe that we can afford to fold our hands, and enjoy our little pleasures and vain amusements and dreamily hope that all will be for the best? Can these terrific forces be adjusted or dispelled without the collision of war, by sitting still and doing nothing? Will not the old enemy inevitably engulf us again, if we do nothing to chain him up?

Nor shall we abolish wars by passing pious resolutions, or having processions against war, or saving ourselves from the torture of hard thinking by subscribing liberally for the relief of those who have suffered from war, or even in the long run by international conferences at Washington or The Hague. All these are good, provided they are recognized as a process of getting up steam for the real thing. Lord Balfour once said to me that he was almost more disturbed by peace movements than by talk about war. "For," he said, "these demonstrations do not deal with the real causes of war. They just put up a paper screen painted to delude the people of good-will all over the world into thinking that something is really being done to prevent war, while in reality behind the paper screen the forces of militarism are sharpening their knives all the time." I shall never forget seeing a United States warship sail into Plymouth harbor in the autumn of 1914, crammed with toys from the children of America for the suffering children of Europe. It was a tender and a kindly thought. But the same people who thus showed their humanity directly the need was there, later found that if the freedom they prized most highly was to be preserved upon the earth, they had to send a vast armada of war vessels to this same port and an army of two million men across the seas.

Today the civilized world is standing in relation to this problem of war exactly where England and America stood in regard to the Great War, before 1914. It is talking about it, but it is not thinking about it. Still less is it doing anything about it. It made a feeble effort in the Covenant of the League of Nations. It has run away even from this slender hope. It has now come back to passing resolutions against the use of poison gas, resolutions which will be just as effective as the resolutions of the Congress of Paris in 1856, which disappeared like snow in the face of the fierce heats of the World War. It is again at its old amusement of building paper screens. Inexorably, all the time, the forces are piling up which years hence will drag new armadas and fresh armies across the waters of the world, in order to save by human slaughter what could be secured by other and better means. The only question is, Is it going to take another and a worse world war to wake the nations up to the necessity of taking action, or are they going to allow wisdom to lead them in time to take the steps necessary to prevent it? To my mind these alternatives are inexorable. The issue is squarely up to us, and if we or our children do drift once more into a world war, we shall have only ourselves to blame.

What is the fundamental cause of war? I do not say the only cause of war, but the most active and constant cause. It is not race, or religion, or color, or nationality, or despotism, or commercial rivalry, or any of the causes usually cited. It is the division of humanity into absolutely separate sovereign states. That humanity should be so divided seems natural, almost a law of nature. That it can ever be otherwise seems almost impossible. Yet it is by all odds the greatest cause of war, and until it is overcome wars as frequent and terrible as those of the past will continue to scourge the earth. In my judgment every movement for the abolition of war which does not recognize this fundamental fact and deal with it, will fail, as every peace movement in the past has failed, because it ignored it.

In order to illustrate what I mean, let us compare the situation in the world today with that which existed in your wild and woolly West in the middle of the nineteenth century. The West was an empty land save for the Indian tribes. Gradually gold-seekers, hunters, traders, prospectors and ranchers began to filter in. There was no law, no state. Every man had to fend for himself. As you can see from reading the pages of Bret Harte, the rights and property of the individual depended fundamentally upon his own strength and courage, and quickness of hand and eye. Quarrels and disputes were frequent, and were settled by bluff or the gun. Power was to the strong. The weak went to the wall. Hold-ups were common, and the "bad man" had a good time until his depredations became so serious that people got together and "did him in."

In such a society peace and freedom are impossible. A number of simple conventional standards grow up, which have some effect in regulating the life of the mining town, conventions rather like international law, dealing with the rules and etiquette of fighting rather than with the prevention of it. But whenever a serious dispute arises there is no machinery for settling it. There are no courts, no legislature to formulate laws, no policemen to enforce them, and either the weak yield to the strong or there is a fight. More than this, there is no basis on which civilized life can be built up or a happy human community arise. Property is insecure. There is no system of title. Contract has no sanction. There is nobody to make roads, undertake sanitation, or conduct education. It is a poor place for women and children. It is a good place only for those who are physically strong and brave.

This state of affairs continues until the scene suddenly changes. There is no more fighting. The "bad man" is quiet or in jail. We see prosperous and progressive communities, busily engaged in agriculture, trade and commerce, secure in their possessions, with great cities, schools and colleges—in fact millions of human beings living contentedly and peacefully together and engaged "upon their lawful occasions." Disputes are settled in courts of law; issues affecting the community are debated on the platform, in the press and in the legislature, and in the end are settled on the basis of a law acceptable to the majority; and the use of violence in private quarrels or in resistance to law is treated as a crime.

What has happened to make the difference? Simply that the inhabitants have taken the steps necessary to dethrone force and to enthrone law and constitutional government in its place. This does not mean that the old grounds of dispute are not there. Men are still greedy and selfish and violent. They still want gold, or land, or perhaps their neighbors' goods. It does not mean that the old issues between progress and reaction, private rights and public well-being are not there. It does not mean that color prejudice or racial feeling or religious differences are any less strong. But it means that these issues are settled by process of law, according to the concepts of reason and justice and liberty current in the community, enforced by the collective strength of the community, instead of by ordeal of battle between the parties, or by the weaker yielding his rights through fear to the strong. And this system of substituting the reign of law for the system of allowing every man to be a law unto himself is the only method by which private war has been stopped and the reign of force has been ended, from the beginning of human history. With the growth of civilization the judgment of the citizens has gradually been substituted for the will of an aristocracy or an autocrat as the law-making power. But everywhere, from the earliest times until today, the only way in which humanity has been able to secure either peace or freedom or the opportunity of progress has been through the substitution of the reign of community law for the reign of individual force, through the agency of the state. Nothing short of this has sufficed, neither conferences, nor methods of conciliation, nor the organization of arbitration. All these things have been tried over and over again. But nothing less than the establishment of the reign of law, binding on every individual, and enforceable by every individual, has ever availed to end war and make civilized progress possible.

The international world today is in the same position as were the western communities seventy years ago. It is without law; every state has to rely for its rights upon its own power; force is supreme. In point of fact, it is in a worse condition, because whereas people in western mining camps were united by constant contact, by the common bond of human association, and by a fairly vigorous public opinion, the international world has no bond of unity at all. Every state is separated from every other state by geography, and usually by language, race and culture, to say nothing of religion and history. In consequence it is animated in its attitude to other communities by ignorance, fear, jealousy, suspicion. It is usually puffed up with pride, selfishness, or ambition about itself. The highest condition to which any state has ever reached is indifference to its neighbor states. Nations often show some love for humanity, and especially for suffering humanity in other lands, but of love by one state for another state there is not, in history, that I can see, a single sign.

In these conditions how is it possible to solve the international disputes involving race, the color line, religion, markets, the control of raw materials, and so on, which continually arise, without war? There are no laws to which to appeal, no representative body to discuss, still less enact, a solution, and no police to forbid violence. Where diplomats fail to agree war is the only redress left.

Some people think that democracy will, in itself, be a preventive of war. Democracy removes some of the older causes of war, dynastic ambition, for instance, and the scheming of military cliques. But it adds a new cause, ignorance. Diplomats can travel and learn about the opinions and rights of other peoples. Democracies cannot. The real difficulty at Paris was not that the statesmen would not agree upon the right course, but that the public opinions of their countries were irreconcilable and out of control. Every democracy is convinced of the justice and reasonableness of its own cause. It easily becomes convinced of the insincerity and designing rapacity of the state with which it differs. There is no real means of explanation. Public opinion gets out of the control of those who know, and the war cloud appears. As a matter of fact, the most effective preventive of war today is not reason or good-will, but fear—the fear of the weak of the consequences of war with the strong, or the fear of the strong of the inevitable cost to itself of war with an equal or even an inferior in strength.

The reason why war has been practically continuous upon the earth's surface from the beginning of time, is that, internationally speaking, we are living like animals in a jungle, with no other means of settling the issues which necessarily arise between us, than the use of tooth and claw. I will give you two or three practical illustrations to show what I mean. Take Europe today. One great cause of war, the existence of the great military autocracies headed by the Hohenzollerns, the Hapsburgs, and the Romanoffs, and the suppression of the freedom of nationalities, which those empires involved—this great cause has been removed. The nationalities of Europe—outside Russia—are absolutely free. They are also all self-governing. But in the process of giving self-determination to the nationalities, Europe has been Balkanized. Let us assume, for a moment, that the difficulties which now confront us over boundaries, reparations, armaments, etc., are successfully overcome, and that national relations become normal once more. Are we any nearer lasting peace? How are some twenty-five states of different sizes, divided by race, language and civilization, occupying one territory which, excluding Russia, is much smaller than the United States, with no means whatever of adjusting the thousand and one questions which must arise between them every hour and every day—how are they going to keep the peace? How are you even going to make them disarm? You may be able to hold back an era of competitive armaments for a few years, but sooner or later one of these states, feeling itself unjustly treated, or impelled by pride or greed, will begin to expand its armaments. The others will inevitably follow suit in self-defense; and then, sooner or later, the competition will end in an explosion as it did in 1914. Can you imagine the forty-eight states of the United States remaining in a very friendly and peaceful condition if they had no Congress, no federal courts, no interstate commerce commissions, no constitution, no laws of any kind, to adjust their relations, and each had a tariff of its own? Yet that is the condition of Europe. And it is also the condition of the world. Is it not obvious that so long as it exists, armaments and wars will exist also?

Take another case. Last year there was some friction between the United States and Japan. Nobody knew quite what it was about. People talked about immigration, and Shantung, and Siberia, and Yap, but it was difficult to point to any very exact matter at issue. Yet the war cloud had begun to form over the Pacific. Opinion in the United States was talking about war. Hard things were said about the Japanese. Observers said that eventually war seemed to be almost inevitable, just as they said that war seemed to be inevitable in Europe for the ten years before 1914. On the Japanese side, too, there had begun to arise the feeling that a struggle was bound to come and that they had better prepare.

The Washington Conference was summoned. Issues were frankly and honestly discussed. It was found that much of the suspicion was unfounded, and an arrangement was reached, which, if it did not solve the underlying problems, got rid of the immediate difficulties, and swept the war-cloud from the sky. But there was nothing between the United States and grave risk of war save successful conference. Suppose the personal equation at the conference had been less statesmanlike. Suppose even that the conference had been delayed and that the bad feeling had been allowed to pile up with all the propaganda of hate and suspicion at full blast. Suppose there had been an accident, an inflammatory speech, an incident like the sinking of the Maine. Do you think that it would have been impossible for a war to break out? And if it had broken out, would not the overwhelming majority of the citizens of both countries have said, "Well, I don't much like this war. But we are in it. The only thing is to see it through"? That would have meant fighting for four or five years. Yet all this happened within three years of the end of the greatest war and the greatest peace movement in history. Am I so very far from the truth when I say that today I can see no security against another world war?

Let me take one other case. What was it that precipitated the Great War? The effective operative cause of the explosion of 1914 was the surrender of Germany to Prussianism, and the failure of its people to take the control of military and foreign policy out of the hands of the Kaiser, his court, his officers, and his diplomats, into their own hands. But what was it that finally swept all Europe into war? It was the military time-table. No sooner did Austria-Hungary begin to mobilize in support of her ultimatum to Serbia than the Russian General Staff felt bound to do the same, in order not to be caught at a disadvantage if the struggle spread. And no sooner did Russia begin to mobilize than Germany felt that she must do so also, for the plans of the German General Staff in the event of a European war were based upon the capacity of the German army to mobilize a few days faster than the French army, and to crush it before the Russians could take the field. Hence the frantic telegrams of the Kaiser to the Czar, imploring and commanding him to countermand the mobilization, once he realized, when it was too late, where the policy of the ultimatum was hurrying with breakneck speed.

Whether the Kaiser or any other responsible man ever deliberately pressed the button to start a general European war, I don't know. Personally, I doubt it. It was the terrible military time-table, the inevitable outcome of Prussian militarism and the division of Europe into a number of rival and separate national states, which made it almost impossible to stop the war once the first fatal step of mobilization had been taken. The Czar could not countermand mobilization unless Austria-Hungary countermanded it. And neither Berlin nor Vienna would countermand, after the fatal ultimatum to Serbia, because to do so would have meant an abject humiliation for the Central Powers far worse than that of Agadir. And so while telegrams flashed and Sir Edward Grey's proposal for conference was on the wires the fateful minutes passed. One after another the nations mobilized. The situation drifted steadily out of control, until finally the German General Staff insisted on marching through Belgium as the straightest road to victory and the only alternative to eventual defeat, and Europe stumbled headlong into a war, for which Germany was best prepared, but which probably no individual deliberately ignited.

That is the sort of situation which must always occur so long as peoples are organized as absolutely independent states. Having no other security for their rights but their own strength, with all states inevitably changing in relative wealth or man power or strength all the time, there will always be a restless uneasiness among some of them that they are falling behind or unsafe. Some ambitious power will begin to increase its armament, or to make alliances. Its neighbors will follow suit in self-defense. Competition will set in. Each will begin to consider what it will do in the event of war. The war offices and admiralties will begin to make plans. Everybody will find that time, taking the offensive, is what matters, to success. The military time-table which precipitated the war in 1914 will reappear. Finally some crisis will arise more difficult than usual. An incident may occur, one nation may mobilize, and before anybody is aware of it, under the pressure of these terrible military time-tables, the nations will be at one another's throats in an agony of doubt and fear.

These three illustrations will, I think, bring home to you the truth of the proposition I am concerned to establish today.

It is the division of humanity into separate states, each owing loyalty only to itself, each recognizing no law higher than its own will, each looking at every problem from its own point of view, and with no machinery whatever for adjusting their conflicting interests save diplomacy and war, which is the fundamental cause of war. It is because of this division that national, and religious, and linguistic, and color differences, practically always have to be solved by recourse to war. You have in the United States, as every country has, both individuals and communities, which are divided by opinion, by race, language, civilization, and color. But they don't resort to war, because there are other and constitutional means of settling their disputes, and war is both forbidden and prevented. As between nations, however, there are no such means, and consequently states do resort to war, because there is in the last resort no other way of settling matters in dispute. So long as this condition of affairs continues it will, I believe, be as impossible to stop international war as it was to stop the Westerners from drawing their guns, before the territories had been organized on the basis of the reign of law. And I venture to predict that, before many months are past, if we go on as we are, we shall see the old competition in armaments, and the old diplomatic combinations, which ended in Armageddon in 1914, beginning again.

In some respects, what I have said here tonight may seem a commonplace. Of course, it may be said, it is true that wars are the result of the people of the world being organized into separate national states. Everybody knows that. But that is not quite what this lecture has set forth. What I have tried to say has been this: That so long as mankind, and specially civilized mankind, remains organized into separate states, wars, and by that I mean world wars, will continue to decimate mankind and to set back civilization, as they have done ever since the fall of the Roman Empire. I believe that every sane man and woman who considers the matter must become convinced that this statement is true, and that you cannot prevent war, you cannot escape war, so long as states insist on being a law unto themselves, and so long as humanity acquiesces in being divided into fragments with no means of adjusting their relations save diplomacy and war.

In a later lecture I shall go on to draw some deductions from that general proposition. Today, in conclusion, I only want to draw your attention to what that statement really means. Between the outbreak of the Great War on July 31, 1914, and the signature of the armistice on November 11, 1918, there were, according to official calculations, more than ten million men killed, mostly in the flower of youth, and more than thirty million wounded. The loss of life since, and especially of child life, through famine, disease and the disorganization of production and supply, nobody has computed, or probably ever will be able to compute. The physical anguish and mental agony entailed by these losses, not so much to those who have died, but among those who have lived and watched others die, helpless to comfort or to save, cannot even be hinted at in words. This Institute is here assembled largely for the purpose of seeing how order can be retrieved out of the chaos left by those four terrible years of war.

Are we really going to allow the tragedy to happen again? It will happen again unless we take steps to prevent it. Yet if we are to prevent it, we shall have to deal not with vague, easy sentiments, but with something which seems to be a very law of our being, the existence of our countries as absolutely independent sovereign states. If what I have said is true, nothing short of this will avail to end war, for it is the fundamental cause of war.

LECTURE II

The Psychological Reason for War

Humanity today is divided into between fifty and sixty independent sovereign states. These states and the human beings they contain must have relations with one another. It is utterly impossible, even if it were desirable, to keep them in separate water-tight compartments. Human beings are continually moving from one state to another. There is a constant and growing interchange of commodities and raw materials. There is the steady permeation of that highest of all social explosives, new ideas, by personal contact, the newspapers and books. Relations exist between these states, whether they want it or not, and it is obvious that with the growth of modern transportation and invention, these relations are going to become more constant and more numerous, affecting every aspect of human life. The question before this century is this: Are the innumerable issues which must continuously arise between these states, issues which concern national rights, commercial progress, the color line, and all the vast complex of human progress and reform—are these issues to be settled by the barbarous and unbusiness-like methods of diplomacy and war, or by some other and better means?

Humanity has worked out a comparatively successful machinery for regulating disputes between individuals, and between communities of individuals, within the state—a constitutional machinery which adjusts them according to reason and justice and fellowship and not by brute force. But so far we have done practically nothing to establish an analogous means of adjusting disputes or the issues of progress and reform between the communities of men organized as states. Force, in its extreme form of war, is still the authorized final arbiter, and reason and justice have no recognized position. Are we going to continue to acquiesce in this state of affairs, and with it, as its inevitable consequence, in constant minor wars and periodic world wars? Or are we going to try to do for the world as a whole what is everywhere done on the sections of the earth's surface, and substitute some more rational and effective system of dealing with disputed issues?

Let us examine what really happened in those new communities of the West, when what Lord Bryce calls the state of nature was replaced by the reign of law. Technically, of course, the federal government of the United States stepped in and organized the area as a territory. It took the whole body of law embodied in the constitution of the United States, in its statutes, in the common law—the vast heritage of centuries of experience and progress—and made it applicable to the area. At the same time it set up a legislative authority to make new laws, a system of courts to interpret them and a police force to enforce them. And in due time, when its inhabitants became numerous enough and organized enough to frame a constitution for themselves, the territory was converted into a state and admitted to the Union.

That is the mechanical process, a process clearly inapplicable to the situation of the world as a whole. But what is the underlying change in moral attitude which makes possible a change from the reign of force to the reign of law? Is it not this, that the inhabitants of what is a lawless area, whether from motives of idealism and love of progress, or from motives of fear and self-preservation, agree to surrender their individual discretion in certain important respects, and to become members of a social community, governed by laws regulating their conduct towards one another, which are enforced by the community on those who would disobey them? In other words, they recognize that they owe a duty to all the other members of the community and not only to themselves, and therefore combine to frame and enforce laws which secure peace, freedom and opportunity on equal terms for all.

Nowhere has the idea which lies at the bottom of the process whereby war is abolished and peace established within a community, been more clearly set forth than in the constitution voluntarily framed by the Pilgrim Fathers in 1620 for the conduct of their new settlement at Plymouth. Immediately after crossing the ocean in the Mayflower and before landing they embodied this idea in the following solemn covenant: We "do by these presents solemnly and mutually in the presence of God, and one of another, covenant and combine ourselves togeather into a civill body politick, for the better ordering and preservation and furtherance of the ends aforesaid" (namely, to plant a colony), "and by vertue hereof to enacte, constitute, and frame such just and equall lawes, ordinances, acts, constitutions, and offices, from time to time, as shall be thought most meete and convenient for the generall good of the Colonie, unto which we promise all due submission and obedience."

This document, sometimes called the first written constitution, sets forth exactly the fundamental idea which underlies all civilized society, the idea which raises the society of men above animal herds, which makes freedom possible, and which brings peace in its train, when properly applied.

I want to note in passing that the "first written constitution" contains no machinery. It simply sets forth the underlying idea which the Pilgrim Fathers recognized as the necessary basis for their life, namely, that they were members of a community, and that this community could only thrive through obedience to laws framed "for the general good." From this basis, however, has been gradually built up the machinery of a modern democratic state, whereby without fighting or war, not only can every conceivable conflict of interest between individuals be settled according to ideas of justice and reason embodied in law, but every question of policy affecting the progress or well-being of the community as a whole, can be determined, after debate and discussion, by constitutional means, by the votes of the citizens, from the standpoint of what they consider to be the "general good" of the commonwealth. The effectiveness of this idea embodied in the solemn covenant of the Pilgrim Fathers, when carried into practical execution, can be seen not merely in the history of the original settlers at Plymouth, but of the millions who now inhabit the Commonwealth of Massachusetts and the Republic of the United States, which have grown out of this and other similar original foundations.

Now let us turn and look at the situation in the world at large. You find that on every atom of the earth's surface inhabited by man, disputes between individuals are settled and war between individuals is prevented on this basis. The only differences are that the machinery for making and enforcing the laws and determining what is the general good is not as yet always controlled by the people at large, but by hereditary autocrats, oligarchies, or other minorities. Why is it that, in contrast to this state of affairs within the state, between states war still stalks brazen and omnipotent throughout the earth?

The reason, as we saw in my last lecture, is that humanity is divided into more than fifty different communities organized as states, with no common machinery for adjusting their disputes. If that, however, were all that is missing, the remedy would be obvious and easy. We should have only to make a federal constitution for the world, and international war would vanish for ever from the earth. But the obvious impossibility of this makes us realize that there is something else than machinery missing. Is it not that the basis as set forth in the Pilgrim constitution is not there? That basis was that each individual recognized that he was part of a community, and owed a duty to all his neighbors. In the international world not only is there no sense of the duty of one state to another, but there is no sense of the nations forming a single brotherhood, and of the necessity of framing "just and equal laws, ordinances, acts, constitutions," etc., for the purpose of protecting and promoting the welfare of the community of men. It is the absence of any effective desire for the "general good" of the whole family of nations which makes us acquiesce in war as being "natural and inevitable," and prevents us from finding a practical means for adjusting disputes by legal and constitutional methods. Until it makes its appearance we shall never, in my judgment, be able to prevent war on the earth.

As a matter of fact, if you talk to any ordinary man or woman of good-will about humanity, he will express interest in it and a desire that it should be happy. I doubt if there is anybody who does not cherish the hope and belief that humanity as a whole will progress, as an abstract proposition, or who would not view with distaste or horror the idea that any section of it should be condemned to stagnation or still more to extermination. But that sentiment only extends to the sociological or humanitarian field. When you turn to politics, it disappears. Politically, every state thinks primarily of itself and of nobody else. Its citizens acknowledge their liability to be taxed for the sake of one another, and their duty to die, if called upon, in defense of one another. They not only admit no such duty as regards humanity as a whole, but they think it right and natural that they should go to war with their neighbors, if the state of which they are members constitutionally decides that they should do so, whether they think the cause is just or unjust.

It is this worship of the national self which causes the inhabitants of every state to be content with limiting their loyalty to their own fellow-citizens, and which prevents the growth of an effective sentiment that the "general good" of humanity must have precedence over the self-interest of any fraction of humanity.

I do not want to be misunderstood as belittling true patriotism or national feeling. The love for one another expressed in the loyalty which citizens of the same country feel for one another, and the manner in which they are willing to subordinate their individual interests to the general good, whether in framing legislation, or in sacrifice for defense, are entirely good. True patriotism is a higher manifestation than racialism or tribalism. It is a good and noble thing. I hope I am a good patriot myself. I trust you are good patriots, too. My only quarrel is that this patriotic feeling stops short at the national frontiers, so that the loyalty and benevolence that citizens feel for such of their fellow human beings as live within a certain line on the map, turns to jealousy, suspicion, or fear of other peoples who live on the other side of that geographical line.

Just consider how absurd that really is. Most people are concerned in some way or other to make things better. The natural friends and allies of the best citizens and the most progressive and sensible people in every community are people of the same type in other lands. The friends of civilization and progress ought to stand together in every land. Yet the effect of our present self-centered statehood cuts right across this line. We in England feel an obligation towards a primitive, backward, possibly criminal, newcomer who has only recently emerged, perhaps, from barbarism, which we do not feel to citizens of the highest type from France or the United States. And you do exactly the same. According to the accepted standards you would admit the obligation to shoot Shakespeare or Wilberforce, the great British abolitionist of slavery, if you met them on the field of battle in war, and we should admit the duty to shoot Emerson or William Lloyd Garrison in similar circumstances, if our countries unfortunately quarrelled, even though everybody knew that the quarrel was caused by the control of the political life of our respective countries by a far inferior and less enlightened type of citizen.

The more you examine it the more, I believe, you will find that it is this narrow national selfishness which is the psychological root of war, just as the division of mankind into separate sovereign states is the mechanical cause of war. It is this self-centered, exclusive patriotism that fills us with suspicion and fear and even hatred of our neighbors. It makes us want all advantages to come to our own state, and view with jealousy every advantage which comes to another state. It estranges us so much from our brothers as to make us think it natural that we should be organized into separate national states, arrogant and self-assertive, armed to the teeth against one another, and bitterly resentful of any suggestion that they ought not to be a law unto themselves. It prevents the growth of that love of humanity as a whole and desire for its well-being, which is the necessary preliminary to the ending of war. Just as the Pilgrim Fathers or the settlers in the West found that the only way in which they could get peace was to settle disputed issues from the standpoint of the "general good" of the whole community and not by a trial of strength or the surrender of the weak to the strong, so the peoples of the world will find that they also will be able to get peace only by rising to the level of settling their disputes from the standpoint of the "general good" of the whole community of men instead of each trying to get its own way. The growth of a world patriotism, not destroying national patriotism, but extending it to include all humanity exactly as national patriotism extends family loyalty to include all fellow citizens, is the necessary preliminary to the creation of any machinery for the ending of war.

In my last lecture I propose to consider how, if the civilized nations develop a sufficient sense that they are members of a single community of nations, war can be abolished between states, as it has been abolished between individuals. Today, I want to show how, even without any formal international organization, the acceptance of the standard of the "general good" of humanity, as opposed to the self-interest of the sovereign states, begins at once to prevent war, and to make progress possible.

I want first of all to examine the question of whether the World War of 1914 was really inevitable, or whether it could not have been prevented.

I don't propose to go into an elaborate discussion

of the immense documentary testimony as to the origin of the war. I simply want to consider the question in very general terms. I explained in my last lecture, how, under the pressure of the Kaiser and the military party, the competition in European armaments set it. It was obvious to every thinking observer that war was brewing. Every year the tension increased, every year the armies and navies grew greater, every year the gulf of fear and misunderstanding grew wider. Every year the military time-table was tightened up. There was no shortage of responsible men who uttered warnings. Yet nothing was really done to prevent the cataclysm, except a frantic effort when it was too late.

Why was that? Was it not because all the great nations of the world were wholly preoccupied with themselves? They did not want to think about the problem, and so long as the danger seemed to affect somebody else rather than themselves, they did not care. Suppose they had been thinking about world progress, would they not have taken steps long before it was too late? Suppose we were to be whisked back now to a time some years before the war, with the knowledge and understanding we possess now, do you think the war would have taken place? Would not the statesmen and the journalists, the publicists, and thousands of plain citizens, have gone to the German people and said, "What are you afraid of? There is no encirclement of Germany going on. Nobody covets what you have got. Your trade and your prosperity are increasing by leaps and bounds. The reason why you are isolated and alliances are springing up against you is that your government, your foreign policy, your army and navy are not under your control, but under the control of an autocrat and a military clique. We don't think that you are seeking world dominion, but we think your rulers have something of the kind in mind. Directly you have taken charge of your national policy for yourselves and ousted the militarists, you will find that our suspicions and our preparations will disappear. But so long as you leave the militarists constitutionally in charge, we are going to prove to you that you cannot succeed, because, however fast you multiply your armaments, we shall multiply them faster."

Do you think there would have been a war if France and England and the United States had said that even as late as 1908, when the defeat of Russia by Japan had removed from Germany the Eastern menace, and before the race of armaments had become too intense? Don't you think that there would have been a German revolution and not a world war? I do. Yet the situation was just as clear to those who had eyes to see, as it is to everybody now. The nations did not see it simply because they were not interested in the rest of the world, because they had no sense of the "general good" of mankind, and were thinking only of themselves. Dante, in the Inferno, reserves almost the worst punishment for those "who were neither for God nor against him, but only for themselves." The hell through which the world has passed is the inevitable consequence of our thinking only of ourselves. Is it to take another world war to force us to think also of one another?

I will take another case—the Peace Conference. It

is the fashion to decry the work of the Paris Peace Conference. I agree entirely with Mr. Cravath, I think it was, who said in a Round Table the other day that when you consider the state of passion and feeling in Europe at the end of a five years' war, when millions of men had been killed and millions of acres had been ravaged, the wonder was not that the peace was so bad, but that there was a peace at all. As a matter of fact, I believe that if you exclude reparations—which dealt with money, the love of which St. Paul wisely said is the root of all evil—history will rate the political decisions of the Paris Conference, imperfect as they were, as an immense advance on the work of any previous international conference.

What was it that enabled the Peace Conference to do its work at all, to steer its way to any sane conclusions amid the passions and intrigues of forty nations none of them understanding one another? Simply this: That in the Council of Four, you had some men at any rate who, despite many defects, were trying to make a peace from the standpoint both of what was just in itself and of what was for the "general good" of the world. They may have made many mistakes and many lapses. I think they did. But they made a real attempt to curb and discipline national passion and ambition within the limits of what was best for the world as a whole. I venture, indeed, to predict that when the time comes for the whole of the minutes of the meetings of the Council of Four to be published for the whole world to read, public opinion will recognize the sincerity of the attempt, and appreciate more clearly the stupendous difficulties with which the

Council had to contend. On the other hand, cannot we all now see that in so far as the Paris Conference was not a success it was precisely because the world point of view did not prevail sufficiently over the selfishly national point of view?

Since 1919 what has happened? Is it not that the world point of view has practically entirely disappeared, and that every nation is scrambling for itself? I am afraid I am now going to say something which some people may not like. But it would be no service to you if I did not tell you the truth, as I see it. The final destruction of the attempt to regulate the terrible difficulties which presented themselves after the war from a world standpoint, and not simply as a conflict of national interests, came from the United States. The most serious blow that the United States dealt to Europe was not so much the rejection of the Covenant of the League of Nations, as the withdrawal of its presence and counsel from the consideration of post-war problems. And it did so, not because it could not get its advice accepted, but for internal reasons of its own. Before the disappearance of the United States the world standpoint was more or less accepted, and in the United States it had an enlightened and far-sighted advocate. But no sooner did it set the pace by leaving the conference table than the unity was broken, and nations openly said that they also had to think first of themselves, and the situation rapidly degenerated to the condition in which you see it now.

In saying this I do not want to suggest for one moment that our troubles in Europe are to be attributed to the United States. They are primarily of Europe's own creation. Nor do I say it in any censorious spirit, for no nation can pretend that it has not been guilty of political crimes in the last few years. Our own record, for instance, in the matter of reparations, is surely black enough. I think I understand, too, the immense difficulties which present themselves to the United States. It is, I confess, an extraordinarily difficult problem which confronts you, namely, that of how you are to play your part as a world power in helping to guide world policy, while avoiding entanglement with the purely internal problems of Europe. But it is none the less a fact, and it is a fact that nobody can dispute, that whereas after the armistice an attempt was made to deal with world problems from a world standpoint, the withdrawal of the United States destroyed all real possibility of remedying the mistakes of the Peace Conference and of solving post-war problems, because the most powerful nation in the world, the nation most disinterested and constitutionally the most advanced, was no longer there, to inspire, to restrain and to guide.

Take the matter a stage further. What is the fundamental difficulty which prevents a settlement of the problems of the time? Is it not that every nation is now looking at them from the standpoint of its own interests and not from that of the common good? In consequence every nation is beautifully clear about what its neighbors should do, but wonderfully dense about what it should do itself. It is inevitable that confusion and chaos should continue, so long as we each think first of ourselves. Yet directly we begin to consider things from the point of view of what will help the whole family of nations, and not primarily from the standpoint of how it affects ourselves, does it not become obvious almost at once what ought to be done, at any rate in broad outline? I am not going to discuss these things in detail, for the proper place to do that is in the Round Tables. I simply ask the question. If you take the reparation question, the debts question, the scandal of the Near East, still more commercial questions, any one of the problems which agitate us now, and look at it for five minutes from the standpoint of what is going to help the world forward most rapidly to prosperity and peace, is not the answer pretty clear? Is not what we need now a return to that world point of view which for the first time in history flickered into feeble life in the Conference of Paris?

Let us take a final case. Let us look for a moment at the future of Europe. What is it that is fundamentally the matter with Europe? Is it not that its people have no sense of their own essential unity, no sense that they can only prosper in friendship and co-operation? Even leaving out of account the momentary difficulties of the time, how can Europe ever have peace, ever be freed from war, so long as each of its twenty-five states looks at every problem from the standpoint of its own self-centered interests alone? It is manifestly impossible. The forty-eight states of America could not have peace if each were entirely independent and each looked at America's problems from its own point of view, and with no thought of the well-being of the United States as a whole. As a matter of fact, they would not think of the problems of America at all. They would be engaged in an endless quarrel with one another about boundaries, railway rates, customs barriers, commercial advantages, and the relative strength of armaments exactly as the nations of Europe are today. The United States is prosperous and at peace because George Washington and Abraham Lincoln saw that the particular interest of every state was best served by subordinating it to the "general good" of the whole, and they insisted, at the cost of immense sacrifice, that they must be and remain a unity. In consequence, the United States, with an area not unlike that of Europe without Russia, with resources not dissimilar, with 100,000.000 people of exactly the same races, nationalities, and religions as Europe, is prosperous, united, and at peace, while Europe, though it has been freed from the military despotisms and is now democratic, is faced with a long era of discord, suffering and possibly war. Is it not obvious to every person in this room that the only final solution of the European problem, the only means whereby peace and concord can ever be reached among the European peoples, is that they should recognize that the "general good" of all its peoples must prevail over the selfish interests of any of its parts, and take the steps necessary to insure that every dispute shall be settled and every problem solved from this wider point of view?

It is exactly the same with the world. The problem there is less urgent. There is in the nature of things far more risk of disputes and war between nations geographically contiguous than between those separated by the sea. But in essence what is true of Europe is no less true of the world as a whole. Harmony and lasting peace will not even come into sight until the civilized powers, at any rate, begin to recognise that their peoples are members one of another, and therefore to adjust political questions, commercial questions, shipping questions, oil and raw material questions, not as a competition between them for advantage or power, but from the standpoint of what will best promote the peace and prosperity of humanity as a whole.

The truth is that the Golden Rule is not a counsel of abstract perfection, or an injunction to lead a hard and mortified existence here for the sake of reward after death. It is not only sound morality, it is good business as well. And it is no less good a guide in international affairs than it is in commercial or private life.

I remember that Mr. Lloyd George, long ago when he was president of the Board of Trade, found that British shipping was suffering because the load line of safety imposed by the British government was higher than that imposed by commercial rivals and was acting detrimentally to British shipping. People urged him to reduce the British load line to the level of his competitors. He refused. He was determined not to reduce the margin of safety, the safety he thought necessary for British sailors, nor was he prepared to ask Parliament to subsidize the companies. He therefore called a conference of the maritime powers and secured a general agreement to a uniform international safety load line. You see his action was good humanity, good patriotism, and good business as well. And I believe it is always so. The more you do unto others as you would that they should do unto you, the easier it is to agree, and the better the results in the long run for everybody.

Is it not obvious that in international affairs it is impossible for nations to secure what they want for themselves alone? Every nation wants freedom and peace, and profitable commercial exchange. No nation can make sure of any of these by itself. Liberty it can only obtain if it is stronger than all comers. Peace it can never be sure of, for somebody else may start a fight. Profitable trade is only possible where other nations can trade profitably also. The nations will find, sooner or later, that the very things that each is seeking for itself, by itself, these three blessings—peace, freedom and prosperity—they can obtain only by combining to secure them for one another.

These illustrations from current affairs will, I hope, serve to strengthen the fundamental proposition which is the subject of this lecture. The ending of world wars by the establishment of machinery whereby international disputes and the problems of human progress can be settled by some less barbarous and more just and effective means than war, depends upon the growth among the civilized nations of the sense that they are themselves members of a larger human community and that the well-being of that larger community must be the standard by which all international questions must be tried and settled. Until that sentiment is general among the most civilized powers, I do not believe that anything really effective can be done to stop war, and that war will continue on the earth in the future as in the past, the great scourge of man. The great obstacle in the way of the growth of this sentiment is the modern religion of national selfishness. This is, in some ways, the most important point. It is always easy to cheer fine sentiments about humanity and peace. The real difficulties appear when we are faced by the fact that in order to realize those ideals we have to sacrifice many precious prejudices and habits of mind which stand in the way.

We are inclined sometimes to think that we have progressed far beyond the standards of the idolaters of old. We read with horror of the human sacrifices to Baal and Ashtaroth, to Dagon and Moloch. But are we really so very far ahead? If it is true that war can be abolished, and peace and order and freedom can be established on earth by relinquishing our national self-centeredness sufficiently to allow the "general good" of humanity to prevail over our several national wills, we must be worshipping something very ugly and very terrible, that it should lead us, generation after generation, to fresh holocausts on the altar of war. Did the gods of old ever exact a toll of human sacrifice like that which was paid between 1914 and 1918? Are the idols which we worship now going to exact this toll again? Their names are not Moloch, or Baal, Dagon or Ashtaroth today. Nor are they Germany, or Italy, or England, or America, for these names stand for great and noble things. Their names are a little different. They are "Deutschland über alles," the "Sacro egoismo Italiano," "Rule Britannia," "America first." It is the idols of national selfishness which set the stage for the last war, and which will set it for another unless we awake to overturn them in time. It is these hideous forms that make kindly men and generous women suspect and hate and finally fight one another; which prevent them from leaping over the barriers of race and language and religion and stretching out the hand of brotherhood and friendship to all mankind; which hinder us from hastening towards that far-off commonwealth of man where war is for ever ended and freedom is for ever secure.

LECTURE III

The Only Road to International Peace

In my previous lectures I have endeavored to prove two propositions, which I believe to be fundamental if we are ever to abolish war from the earth. The first was that the most potent and constant cause of war, the cause which infinitely outweighs all others, is the division of humanity into absolutely independent sovereign states. I tried to show that in contradistinction to the situation within the state, there was, in the international sphere, no legal or constitutional machinery for adjusting, according to reason and justice, the disputes which arise from other and more immediate causes, such as national ambition, commercial rivalry, color prejudice, the advance of civilization, etc., and that in consequence resort was necessarily made from time to time to war, as the only final court of appeal. The second proposition was that we should never be able to create any effective machinery for adjusting international issues by legal or constitutional means, and so abolish war, until the civilized nations had overcome their narrow self-centered nationalism sufficiently to recognize that they belong to the larger community of all nations, and that international issues ought to be settled from the standpoint of the welfare of the whole, and not as a conflict between the self-interest of the parts.

Nations today are far from being ready to admit

this conclusion. But assuming that they were, what practical steps would be necessary to make an effective end of international war? That is the question I propose to discuss today.

It must be obvious to all that the only method is the substitution of the reign of law over all nations, for the present reign of force. Nothing short of that will suffice. Obedience to law or principle is the condition of peace, freedom and happiness, in every sphere of life. No musician can make progress until he obeys the law of harmony. No individual is either really at peace or free until he submits himself to the wisdom of the Ten Commandments. No community is at peace or free in which the citizens do not submit themselves to the restraints of their country's constitution and laws. The Pilgrim Fathers saw that very clearly. And nations, similarly, will be neither at peace nor free until they unite to bring themselves under the reign of just law.

Mere benevolence will never keep the peace among the nations, any more than it will keep the peace among individuals—in their present state of moral growth—without the restraint of obedience to law, and without the machinery whereby disputes can be settled impartially according to law, and fighting is prohibited and prevented. If law is indispensable in the civilized community of the Commonwealth of Massachusetts, what reason have we for thinking that it is not even more necessary among the estranged and suspicious communities of men? If nations cannot trust one another enough to unite to frame a means of settling disputes according to justice, what possible ground is there for thinking that they will always manage to settle them by voluntary agreement? As William Penn said, "Government is the means of justice, as justice is the means of peace."

We have not got to wait till man has realised perfection before we create the machinery of the reign of the law. When he is perfect he won't need it. It is precisely because he is still imperfect, quarrelsome, selfish, greedy, intolerant, that it is needed at all. You don't suppose that all the citizens of the United States or Great Britain are perfect. There are fairly good specimens of both human perfection and human depravity in both countries. Yet we all know that we could not get on at all without the machinery of law. We know also that it is the less good citizens who need it most and who have to resort to it most often. Political mechanism is not a symptom of perfection. It is the means whereby a community insists that quarrels between imperfect individuals, or disputed questions of public policy, be settled by legal and constitutional means, and not by the method of fighting, which is both bad for the parties concerned, and upsets and damages the rest of the community as well. It is just the same with nations. They are certainly imperfect, and it is because they are still imperfect that they need some constitutional means of solving their disputes if they are to avoid war.

Hence, I can reach no other conclusion, whether from a study of the past, from experience of the present, or from the consideration of theory itself, than that war between states will continue until we apply to the world as a whole the same fundamental ideas as are universally applied within the state. War will only be abolished from the earth when the peoples of the world, or at any rate the civilized peoples, combine under some organic constitution whereby international questions are settled by an appeal to law designed to promote international justice, law which is obeyed and enforced by all mankind, until it can be modified by constitutional means. That is the basis of peace and civilized government everywhere in democratic communities today. In my judgment it is the only means whereby peace and civilized government can take the place in world affairs of the unintelligent, barbarous, and destructive method of war. That, to my mind, is the inexorable teaching of underlying principle. I do not believe that it is possible to escape it.

Before going on to consider the practical application of this conclusion, let us consider for a moment the alternatives which are usually put forward. Take first of all disarmament. The agitation for disarmament, in so far as it represents the rebellion of public opinion against a new race of competitive armaments, is entirely to the good. I would not lift a finger to discourage the campaign. On the contrary I would help it in every way, unless it were represented as a final solution in itself. It is a step in the right direction. But it does not solve the problem. No nation can or will abandon its armaments altogether until it has both an alternative method of protection and a system in which it has confidence whereby disputes with its neighbors can be justly and honorably decided. Universal peace will never come from universal disarmament. You would not have got very far with giving peace and real freedom to the western communities of the United States if you had simply taken away the guns of individuals and done nothing more. Until the institutions of a state were established, there was no other way of settling disputed questions than fighting, and if individuals who felt themselves unjustly treated or aggrieved, had not been able to use guns they would have used clubs or their fists, or any weapon to their hands, to defend what they believed to be their rights. It is exactly the same with nations. They cannot and they will not disarm without an alternative system of protection and of settling disputes. You would not do so yourselves. And if there is no alternative system, nations will, sooner or later, be landed in war. If they are not united enough to form a common machinery for the conduct of their common affairs, it is a pure delusion to think that they will be able to escape disagreements or to avoid settling those disagreements by fighting.

Disarmament, therefore, is no solution. What about the international court? This also is a step in the right direction, for it accustoms men to think of justice as the true arbiter of international problems. But international courts by themselves cannot suffice. Courts of law interpret law, adapt law to the changing facts of human life, develop law; they do not enact it. That is the function of the legislative body. If the courts began to enact laws they would immediately become the center of violent controversy, just as legislatures are today. Their impartiality would be assailed, their authority would wane, and their decisions would be disregarded. The function of the judiciary is quite distinct from that of the legislature. The latter is representative of the community, discusses its problems, and gradually embodies in a law the best solution it can, which is binding on all the citizens and enforced by the courts. The courts themselves have no responsibility for the wisdom or unwisdom of the law. They are solely concerned with its practical application. No body of a judicial or unrepresentative character could possibly solve the vast problems relative to the color line, to the development of self-government among backward peoples, to the control of world markets and supplies of raw materials, which are increasingly going to convulse mankind. These are political matters, not judicial, and they must be settled by political means.

What about the system of international conference, either temporary, like the Washington Conference, or permanent, like the League of Nations? I am not, of course, going to discuss the merits or demerits of the present League, for that is a matter of party politics in the United States. Nor is it material to my point to do so. I entirely endorse the underlying idea of a League or Association, call it what you will, of all the nations of the earth, to deliberate about world problems. Some such regular institution is essential to international understanding and without it no progress whatever towards world peace can be made. But no such body can, in itself, end war. At the very highest it can only do what your Confederation did between 1781 and 1789. It will ultimately fail to solve the international problem for exactly the same reason as the Confederation failed to solve the American problem. The Confederation failed because, its members being delegates, it tended to approach every issue as a matter of adjusting the conflicting interests of separate states, and not from the standpoint of what was best for the American people as a whole. It failed still more because even when it could agree upon the wise solution it could not give effect to it, because its decisions were only effective if they were simultaneously accepted and carried out by thirteen separate legislatures, widely scattered, and each looking at the question from its own point of view. As you all know, the system broke down hopelessly, as it has broken down in Canada, Australia, South Africa, Germany, everywhere where it has been tried, and a federal system had to be erected in its place. It will be exactly the same with a League or Association of all nations. It is a step in the right direction. But a League or Association of absolutely independent sovereign nations will ultimately fail, partly because its members will be delegates and forced to discuss world problems as a matter of bargaining between their separate states, and partly because even when it can reach unanimity, its conclusions, however good, will never be accepted or carried out simultaneously by more than fifty separate states, scattered all over the world, and wholly immersed in their own point of view.

I think every dispassionate thinker will agree that none of these expedients, admirable as they are, as steps in international co-operation, can ever, by themselves, end war. I would go further. Unless people see clearly what is the ultimate goal and recognize that these methods are just steps towards that goal, they may become that dangerous thing, the paper screen. They send the world to sleep; they make it think that it is dealing with the real causes of war, whereas it is not, so that eventually it finds itself suddenly awakened, as in 1914, to the horrible reality by the shriek of the bullet and the roar of the guns.

I don't want to be misunderstood as being against international co-operation. I am for it, to the limit, in every helpful form. It is the only present practical method of reaching agreement and diminishing the risk of war. All I am concerned with today is to point to what I believe to be the fundamental truth, that the only method of finally ending war, and therefore of establishing freedom for all nations on the earth, is to apply to the world as a whole the same fundamental ideas which have alone given peace and liberty and opportunity in its separate parts.

I venture to believe that the great majority of those who have considered the arguments and facts set forth in these lectures will agree in theory with this conclusion. The real difficulty is to see how to convert that theoretical proposition into a practical and effective reality.

Before I go further, however, I want to make it clear that I am not talking practical politics. I am for the moment a political theorist. The ending of war along the lines I have been discussing is not a matter of practical politics today. Nor will it be for many years. We are still in the thinking stage. The question will have to be thought out far more deeply than I have done, and in many countries, before the idea can enter the field of practical realities. I discuss this somewhat abstract subject here because the Institute of Politics in Williamstown is an organization which exists not for partisan or propaganda purposes, but for the scientific study of international affairs. And it is only by hard thinking in such institutes that we shall ever reach conclusions which are practical and not merely theoretic. I should like to say in passing that I think the Institute is the most interesting experiment of its kind in the world, for it is the only institution that I know of which brings real students together, free from party bias, with access to governmental knowledge, but free from governmental control, with direct contact with representatives of foreign opinion, for the purpose of collective, creative thinking about the international problem.

If you think I am going to give you a nice, clear-cut, neatly docketed proposal for preventing war, all tied up with string, and embodied in a draft treaty or convention, I'm afraid you will be disappointed. The people who begin that way, in my experience, end nowhere. I am simply going to throw out for consideration a few leading ideas, which, in my opinion, go to the root of the problem, and which may help those who want to do some pioneer thinking about this great question, to think towards an ultimately practical proposal. My ideas are all tentative, and they will not become definite and conclusive until they have been discussed and criticized by others. I hope, therefore, that you will take what I am now going to say, not as the advocacy of a plan, but as a contribution to thought upon a great problem. For it is only by thinking, and thinking together, that we shall ever solve it.

You will remember that in referring to the "first written constitution" of the Pilgrim Fathers, I noted the fact that it contained no machinery for giving effect to the fundamental covenant of the original settlers that they would enact and obey laws designed to promote the "general good" of the community. The precise machinery for giving effect to this idea was a later and a gradual development. I think we must approach the world problem in the same way. The first indispensable step is to get general assent to the fundamental covenant that the world is a single community of many nations, that the promotion of the "general good" of humanity ought to be the standard of our national conduct, and that if we can find the way to do so, we ought, to quote the Pilgrim Fathers again, "to enact such just and equal laws, ordinances, acts, constitutions and offices, from time to time, as shall be thought most meet and convenient for the general good" of mankind, and that to these we ought to "promise all due submission and obedience."

I don't think that anybody in this hall who thinks about the matter will dissent from the view that we ought, if it is practically possible, to make the welfare and progress of the world as a whole the object of our international policy and action. Let us assume, therefore, a general desire on the part of civilized peoples to drop their self-centeredness and rise to the level of being willing to combine to promote the welfare of humanity, and incidentally, of course, of their own countries as part of it. Is it possible to reproduce on a world scale the three institutions whereby the reign of law has been established, and warfare abolished, within each state? Is it possible to create a world legislature representative of the people, to enact the laws for the general good of the world, world courts to interpret them, and a world police force, backed by some kind of military or militia force, to enforce them?

Before trying to answer that question, let us face up, honestly and squarely, to the difficulties. We shall make no progress to the goal of world law and world peace unless we do so.

The first obstacle which we meet is the enormous difference in race, language and culture among civilized nations. The basis of every civilized and democratic community with the normal institutions of a state, as above, is a substantial similarity among the citizens. They usually all speak the same language, or are willing to do so. They are usually at about the same level of civilization, or anxious to reach it. They are all either of one nationality, or are assimilable to that nationality, and anxious to be assimilated to it. Where there is no probability of assimilation, immigrants are excluded.

There is no such similarity even in the civilized world. The great national entities of the world—France, Italy, Britain, the United States, Germany, Russia, Japan—all differ profoundly. You could not get them to merge their national identities in a single cosmopolitan state. They ought not to do so, even if they could. That form of internationalism looks backward and not forward. There is no possibility, and in my judgment ought to be no possibility, of creating a world state on the model of any national state which now exists. The nations are the pillars of the world's temple of peace. Nothing less strong will support the roof which is still to be built.

The second obstacle is no less formidable, and that is the different levels of civilization. The great majority of humanity is still not yet self-governing in any real sense of the word. If you look at it, Asia, as a whole, is not, though it is marching fast in that direction. The overwhelming majority of the four hundred millions of China and the three hundred and fifteen millions of India, though self-governing institutions are making their appearance in both, as yet take no conscious interest in the problems of government. The politically minded and the electorate capable of casting an intelligent vote are still only a tiny fraction of the whole population. When you turn to Africa or Polynesia you see that most of their inhabitants, so far from being able to govern themselves when subjected to contact with the terrible stresses and temptations of the modern world, still require the protecting and guiding hand of a highly civilized power.

It is obvious that world organization on a democratic basis for all humanity is still far off. The civilized nations will not allow their own future, and the future of the world, to be controlled by the votes of peoples who have not yet demonstrated their practical capacity to conduct an orderly and progressive government of their own countries. It would not help the progress of the world if they did.

Then there is a third obstacle. That is the sheer problem of numbers. The population of the world is about 1,700,000,000 people, and if one third of these are children, a world assembly on the basis of one member for every 100,000 electors would exceed 10,000 members, a wholly fantastic and unworkable number. The present machinery of democracy does not seem to be very appropriate for dealing with the world problem.

Then there is a fourth obstacle. If ever the world is to have unity and liberty and peace, it must be on the basis of the self-government of all its parts. Over and over again in history great leaders have attempted to give mankind some respite from war, and the set-backs to progress that war entails, on an autocratic basis, and they have always failed. The only successful attempt was that of Imperial Rome, which, for several centuries, gave the civilized world the only universal peace it has ever known. But in changing from a republic to an empire, Rome destroyed the mainspring of its vitality. Its administration became more and more lifeless and inflexible. Its peoples, having no responsibility for their government or their laws, became effete. And finally it collapsed under the pressure of barbarian invasion from without, and moral decay within. Charlemagne tried to restore it in 800 A. D. The Papacy tried to establish a universal theocracy under Innocent III. Napoleon tried to set up a universal empire a century ago. Some German minds even thought of it in 1914. But great as were the blessings which universal peace offered to mankind, it preferred freedom more. Every time that a universal empire was in sight nations rebelled, and the attempt was foiled. National self-government is the only foundation upon which world unity and world peace can rest.

I think that is a fair statement of the chief practical difficulties, though there are many others. There is, in particular, that most imposing, but least substantial obstacle of all, the sheer inertia of humanity itself, and its prejudice against reform. The mere enumeration of these difficulties shows how formidable a proposition we are up against, and how inappropriate is the simple mechanism of an ordinary democratic national state to their solution.

How then can we proceed? I think we can only proceed along the same line of development which has succeeded so well in the past. I wish I had time to discuss the political system established by Moses and the Israelites as recorded in the Bible. That to my mind is the beginning of self-government, and of his idea of the commonwealth. But I will begin with the Greek city state, which invented democracy as we know it—that is to say, the system whereby the laws under which a community lived and its executive were made amenable to popular control. Greece perished because under its primitive democratic system the city state was limited to the number of citizens who could hear the voice of a single orator, and so vote on the issues at stake. Greece was therefore divided into a great number of city states which had no means of adjusting their common affairs, rather like civilization today. They were constantly at war, and the Greek political system perished from internecine strife, ending in conquest from Macedonia.

Then came Rome. Rome developed the concept of

the universality of law, and out of this idea and the intense patriotism of the city of Rome grew up a system which eventually embraced the whole civilized world, and kept the peace for centuries within it. But as we have seen, Rome failed to invent a system for extending responsibility to her citizens once the reign of her laws extended far beyond her city walls. She became an empire, and, like Greece before her, perished from internal decay and external attack.

Then England invented the representative system. This advance meant far more than a mere change in mechanism. It implied a vast moral advance in the sense of brotherhood and loyalty on the part of the individual. Without that moral advance—an advance, in my judgment, only made possible by Christianity—modern parliamentary government would have been impossible. The representative system not only brought into being states which extended over an immensely larger area than the Greek city states, but saved them from internal decay because it made all citizens responsible for the laws under which they lived.

Finally America invented federalism—the division of the functions of government between local and central legislatures—a still further advance both in mechanism and moral outlook. Federalism has made it possible to extend responsible constitutional democratic government over a whole continent, as Australia following the American precedent has been able to do. And I should like to remind you in passing how France, inspired by this example, not only established the democratic system on the western end of

Europe, but under Napoleon, in his earlier and creative period, swept away the medieval system of Central Europe, and so paved the way for modern European democracy.

But even federal democracy as we have known it, despite all recent developments in transportation and telegraphic communication, is not really applicable to the world as a world. I have already pointed out some difficulties. But does federation do anything to point the way? I think, in its American form, it does.

There are three fundamental ideas underlying the American Commonwealth which seem to me of vital moment. First, the sovereignty of the Constitution, which, for practical purposes, can only be altered by the people themselves. Secondly, the definition of the powers of the federal and state governments in the Constitution, so that no government has the right to exercise any authority over any other. And third, the vesting of the duty alike of interpreting and enforcing the Constitution, not in the governments, but in the courts, both state and federal. What does this mean? It means that so long as the people of the United States as a whole give effective support to the Constitution and the courts, there can never be a collision between any of its governments. The Convention which drew up the Constitution saw that to give the power of enforcement to any government as against any other government, inevitably involved war, and it consequently provided that the Supreme Court should have jurisdiction over all controversies between states. In other words, under the American Constitution, no controversy between states, or between the Federal Government and the state government, is at present conceivable which is not a matter for judicial determination and settlement. And where the development of the Constitution by judicial decision is inadequate or unsatisfactory, the Constitution can be amended by the people themselves.

While these ideas may not be applicable in their entirety to the world problem, they seem to me to point the way. Is it impossible that we should be able to draw up a constitution for the world which would define the rights and duties and independence of all national states, which would set up some body to deal, from a world standpoint, with those matters which today lie outside the control of any nation, and which by vesting the enforcement of the constitution in the courts of every country, supplemented by an international court, would end the possibility of international war, so long as the peoples were willing to give effective support to the constitution itself?

It has been said that I am advocating a super-state. If you mean by that a body which can give orders to the United States or Great Britain, or France or Russia, I emphatically am not. That way failure and disaster lie. Within their own spheres the Congress of the United States, the Parliament of Britain, the Legislature of France, must remain omnipotent and supreme.

But is there any reason why you in this room should not be citizens, in the constitutional sense, of the city of Boston, of the state of Massachusetts, of the Republic of the United States, and of the commonwealth of all nations? If you were, would you be any less free and independent? The body which represented you in your capacity as a citizen of the world would be no more able to interfere with the United States than the United States is able to interfere with the Commonwealth of Massachusetts. Each would have the organs necessary to enable it to deal with its own affairs. But there would be no ground for dispute or war between the national states of the world, because the duty of dealing with the matters which lie outside national control, and which today are dealt with by diplomacy and war, would then be constitutionally controlled by some body whose business it was to act as trustee for human welfare as a whole. I am not in favor of a super-state, but I am in favor of seeing whether the civilized nations cannot enter into a constitutional bond which will give justice, liberty and equal opportunity to all peoples. If a constitution could be created, it would end in one stroke imperialism, international rivalry, disputes about boundaries and half the issues which are now regularly settled by war.

Leaving on one side prejudice and inertia, what are the difficulties in the way of proceeding along these lines? The first and most obvious is, that it involves a curtailment of national sovereignty, or, rather, it means a definition of a line of demarcation between the powers to be exercised by the body representing people in their national capacity, and those exercised by the body which represents them in their capacity as world citizens. But I ask you to consider this: Do sovereign national states really exercise sovereignty in the world sphere now? They manifestly do not. War is not sovereignty, and that is the only power they can exercise as sovereign states. In 1781 the peoples of Massachusetts and New York thought that they were sovereign powers in America. George Washington and Alexander Hamilton explained to them that they were not. It was no exercise of sovereignty for the thirteen states to quarrel and fight about America's future. The only way in which the people of America could exercise sovereignty was, while remaining divided into thirteen states for local affairs, to become a single people for common affairs. Then, and only then, were they able to exercise sovereignty—that is, to control American affairs—for then, and only then, could they create the constitutional organs which enabled them to do so. Between 1781 and 1789 the people of America, despite their independence of Great Britain, were not free, for they could neither agree nor act about anything. After 1789 they were free and had dominion, because they had brought themselves under the reign of a single sovereign law.

It is exactly the same with the world. The peoples of the world today are neither sovereign nor free, in any real sense of the word. Their only power is to fight, and that is not freedom. They cannot control the world in which they live. The only way in which they can become free and become sovereign is to pool their sovereignty, so to speak, in that sphere which lies beyond national rights, and create an organism, responsible to themselves, through which they can control world issues by law, instead of by the savage and often meaningless means of war.

Further: Is not the universal tendency towards centralization of government, and away from the true democratic idea, is not the delay in the spread of democracy itself in the world, largely due to the fact that every nation has to base its constitution and its methods on the risk of war? The liability to war is the great centralizer, the greatest empire builder, the great enemy to democracy, in the world. We shall only be able to establish a true constitutional balance in our own countries when constitutional government within is balanced by constitutional government without.

The second difficulty which arises is this: What about nations which may not wish to join such a system, and prefer or are only fit to remain in a state of nature outside? And what about the non-self-governing peoples? How can they share in sovereignty and exercise its responsibilities? As to nations who refuse, or are too lawless, to join, is it not possible to begin to bring unity into the world on these lines gradually, by introducing the system first among as many peoples as will unite to submit themselves to the reign of law, as it was introduced first along the Eastern seaboard of America, and later gradually extended until it included and gave peace and order to the whole of the United States? The possibility is worth considering anyway. And as to the backward peoples the process is clear. The American Constitution makes provision for territories. You can deal with the Philippines. Sovereignty can be vested theoretically in the whole people of the world, but in the intermediate stages, until civilization and self-government have made more progress, the most advanced peoples can act in world affairs, as they do today, as trustees for the whole, under proper constitutional guarantees.

Finally, there is the difficult question of mechanism. How are you going to constitute a body which can speak for humanity in the extra-national sphere? Here it seems to me that we await another advance in political mechanism of the same kind as that made, first by the Greeks, then by the British, and then by America. You have got to discover a development beyond both the representative and the federal systems, if you are to create an institution which can really be said to represent humanity, which will secure the confidence of humanity to the extent that they will entrust it with the decision of extra-national affairs, and which in some way can claim the allegiance of the individual. I do not see why that new idea should not emerge here in America, among those who created and understand best the last great constitutional invention. Anyhow, I put it up to you to discover it!

As I have pointed out before, however, far more than a mere change in mechanism is involved. It means a profound advance in moral outlook. It implies that a sufficient proportion of humanity come to see that they owe a loyalty to all men, of the same kind as they feel that they owe to their fellow nationals. The members of each nation have to relinquish the idea that they are in competition or rivalry, and feel that they can be citizens in both the nation and the world, and that there is no rivalry between them. As a matter of fact, if the leading nations of the world really recognized the brotherhood of all men, and thought about justice and human welfare and not only about themselves, would it take very long for them to unite sufficiently to put an end to all risk, at any rate of the kind of internecine wars with which we are threatened today? I do not think they would find the difficulties insuperable.

This change in spirit and outlook is the fundamental thing. As it appears, everything else will be comparatively easy—the distribution of powers, finance, boundaries, armaments—for it is always possible to find means of giving practical form to an effective general will.

That is as far as I can go today. I believe you will find that some of these ideas are fruitful and that if you study them they will lead you further than may at present appear. I would only suggest two broad subjects for further study. On the one side I think you will find the fundamental ideas involved in the problem more clearly enunciated and discussed in the writings and speeches of your own fathers than anywhere else. If you study the works and lives of George Washington, Thomas Jefferson, Alexander Hamilton and the other writers in "The Federalist," John Marshall and Abraham Lincoln, you will, I believe, be driven to the same fundamental conclusion as I have been, that only by means of some organic structure of the kind I have discussed, will you ever be able to abolish war from the earth.

On the other hand, I think you will find that it will repay you to study the constitutional theory, and, still more, the practice and spirit of the modern British

Commonwealth. It contains within itself a quarter of the people of the earth. It unites in one loose bond, completely independent self-governing nations, and peoples of every race and color, and level of civilization. Its institutions are very rudimentary. But they serve to keep the peace, and to promote freedom among 440,000,000 of the children of men. The British Commonwealth, indeed, shows that the idea of world unity is not so far-fetched as at first appears, and involves far less interference and change in the existing national system, than people believe.

I see that somebody has suggested that I want the United States to join the British Commonwealth. That is absurd. It is not a question of either entity joining the other, but of their combining with other nations to give some kind of constitutional system to this world. As a matter of fact, in my judgment, the British Commonwealth cannot indefinitely last in its present form. If the world progresses towards unity and peace, it will be replaced by a greater thing. If the world moves back again, it will break up in that further Balkanization of mankind, and that still more frightful world war, which are inevitable if the civilized peoples do not read in time the lessons of the last ten years.

I have an idea that a good many people are saying: "Well, the total abolition of war is a beautiful dream, but it is only a dream. Some day it may be possible, but not now." To this I would make two answers. The first is that the main burden of these lectures is not to advocate this plan or that, but to point out that we are faced with two alternatives, and two only—

steady constructive progress in the direction of world unity, and another world war. We can have whichever we choose. But the choice itself is, in my judgment, inexorable. If we sit still and murmur, "Well, it's a beautiful dream, but we cannot do anything about it now," then we are in fact casting a vote for another world war.

The second answer is, that I believe that the ending of war by these means is ultimately perfectly feasible. The road may be long and difficult. It will certainly wind up hill all the way. But it is none the less the road. What is it that really stands in the way of moving, and moving steadily forward? Is it not fundamentally fear, prejudice, ignorance, inertia, and self-centeredness? There is nothing really impossible about creating the constitutional machinery whereby civilized humanity can deal with the problems of the earth by some more intelligent and humane method than war. The problems are there. They have got to be dealt with. The only question is whether we shall go on failing to deal with them because we can only fight about them, or whether we shall create some means whereby we can deal with them according to reason and justice and from a human point of view. To face this question, and not to ignore it, is, to my mind, to have one's feet on the ground.

In the Epistle to the Hebrews, St. Paul says that "Faith is the substance of things hoped for, the evidence of things not seen." The substance of world unity is certainly not seen yet. Is it not, therefore, faith that we need now, the vision that the Founder of Christianity said could remove mountains, not so much of rock, but of prejudice, and fear, and ill-will?

I have taken as the subject of these lectures "The Prevention of War." But I do not think that the desire to avoid war is the best or the most potent motive which ought to guide us. I doubt if we shall ever abolish war simply because we want to avoid it. The only power that will gird us with the needed strength is a consuming desire to see a better, cleaner, happier world, a world not desecrated and ruined and set back in its progress by recurrent bloodshed and destruction.

If we can only lift ourselves out of the rut of our own national prepossessions and selfishness, and go up on to a mental mountain and survey humanity and its problems as a whole, does not our course seem clear? We see our fellow human creatures, men and women and children, just like ourselves, with the same virtues, the same failings, the same striving for better things, the same human hearts. We see some comparatively wise and thoughtful, fortunate and prosperous. We see others ignorant and thoughtless, in misery and squalor. In some areas of the earth we see civilization and progress. In others we see pools of phosphorescent decay just stirring with new life. Yet everywhere there is not co-operation for improvement, but jealousy and strife and war. Is it not obvious that we can none of us really progress until we combine to drain these disease-breeding pools, with education and true knowledge, and to build human ties and constitutional bridges uniting all races and nations. Are we not in reality, all one people?

It is really a great adventure which lies before us, if we have eyes to see it. It is an adventure calling for even greater qualities than those needed for fighting a war. There is no risk of our becoming effete if we really attempt it. And it is for the civilized peoples to take the lead.

There are some lines written by Sir Owen Seaman early in the Great War, which caught very well the spirit in which nine hundred and fifty thousand of the varied races and peoples of the Commonwealth to which I belong, laid down their lives for freedom's cause. The copy which I first saw was found upon the body of an Australian soldier who had come thirteen thousand miles to fight in Flanders fields. They embody, I think, the spirit in which your sons also crossed the seas. They set forth the spirit in which alone we can make sure that the work which they died to begin, that no such tragedy should happen to humanity again, shall not be left unfinished, because of anything that we leave undone.

"You that have faith to look with fearless eyes
Beyond the tragedy of a world at strife,
And trust that out of night and death shall rise
The dawn of ampler life;

"Rejoice, whatever anguish rend your heart,
That God has given you, for a priceless dower
To live in these great times and have your part
In Freedom's crowning hour.

"That you may tell your sons who see the light
High in the heavens, their heritage to take:—
'I saw the powers of darkness put to flight;
I saw the morning break!' "

BY

LIONEL CURTIS

LECTURE I

The Union of South Africa

LIKE Dr. Garfield, I turn to salute the great figure that stood in this place last year. I have always known that James Bryce was liked and admired in America, but till I came to Williamstown I never realized how you loved him, and why. It was, no doubt, because he loved, and, what is more, respected the American people. But there was more in it than that. When I asked a friend here why he counted so much with you he answered: "Because he was the first man who told us the truth about our municipal government." That again does not cover the whole ground; but it was, I believe, his love of truth and its fearless utterance that largely endeared him to the people of this country. You are in danger of making me believe that hardly any one here was quite so beloved as this fellow countryman of my own. Forgive me for saying this, for exactly the same is true of at least two American ambassadors to London in recent years. Friends are sometimes dearer than brothers.

Bryce achieved more than most politicians in the sphere of practical politics; but they occupied the least important part of his life. To him the experience he gained in them was raw material from which to extract knowledge. Up to the last minute he was busy interpreting facts for the guidance of those that would follow him. Here in Williamstown his footprints are fresh, and I will try to tread in them by telling you of two national movements in which I happen to have been engaged. One was a movement to achieve responsible government in South Africa, the other an attempt to initiate responsible government in India. In a third lecture I shall try to convey to you a view on international affairs formed from experience of these and other national movements.

To explain the South African question I must try to tell you how it arose. In the Middle Ages a valuable overland trade between Asia and Europe was developed in spices—products precious enough to be carried by camels to Constantinople. From Constantinople they were distributed through Europe for sale to the classes rich enough to pay for such luxuries. In the fifteenth century the routes of this trade were cut by the fall of Constantinople and the rise of the Turkish Empire. To revive this trade it became a matter of primary interest to the merchants of those days to find some route to India by the sea which was not open to interruption by the Turks. In quest of such a route Columbus stumbled upon this continent. In 1497, the problem was solved by the enterprise of a Portuguese captain, Vasco da Gama, who rounded the Cape of Good Hope, reached the coast of India, and announced that he had come to bring Christianity and take away spices. The whole empire of the East was then granted to Portugal by a Papal Bull, and for close on a century the wealth of the Indies was brought to Europe in Portuguese ships.

Just as coaling stations are necessary now, so in those days, owing to the prevalence of scurvy in sailing ships, some port at the half-way house in South Africa, where the ships could call for fresh water and vegetables, was a vital necessity. A glance at the map of the world will show you that the toe of Africa is the obvious place; and if you will look closely you will see how few harbors in South Africa there are. The ideal half-way house is Table Bay. By one of those strange accidents which divert the course of history, the Portuguese never occupied this harbor. A party landed in full armor, but, too heavy to maneuver, were slaughtered by Hottentots, who doubtless mistook them for large crustaceans. So the Portuguese always fought shy of this spot and made their stations at Algoa Bay, where Port Elizabeth now is, and at Delagoa Bay on the east coast, neither of which is comparable in strategic importance to Table Bay.

Up to the year 1580 the produce of India brought to Lisbon by Portuguese ships was distributed to the rest of Europe by Dutch merchants and shipping. In that year Portugal was annexed to Spain, with which the Netherlands was at war. Lisbon was thus closed to the Dutch, who determined to embark on the Indian trade for themselves and to carry the conflict with Spain into the East. With these objects in view the Dutch East India Company was incorporated. In 1651 the Dutch East India Company under Van Riebeck founded a colony at Table Bay and called it Kaapstad. The city, now known as Cape Town, is surrounded by the ramparts of Table Mountain, the dominating feature of a peninsula connected to the mainland by a spit of sand thrown up by the sea. The summit, five thousand feet above the town, is flat, and the prevailing wind from behind it condenses in a cloud which waves like the folds of a gigantic tablecloth above the city, and rushes in cataracts down the gorges. When the sun turns it to molten gold it is even as though the glory of the Lord descended on the tabernacle. That mountain with its southern promontory, the Cape of Good Hope, was the turning-post in a race for the empire of the East.

The Company, however, had no interest in the place except as a port of call on the way to India. All they wanted from the Cape was water and fresh vegetables for the use of the ships. The local Hottentots were useless as laborers, so the Company imported Malay slaves to cultivate the gardens, and to this day their descendants continue to form an important element in the population of Cape Colony. The three principal levels of human society, the European, the Asiatic, and the African Native, took root in the country side by side. South Africa thus became a microcosm in which human problems can be studied as a physicist studies the forces of nature in the test-tubes of a laboratory. The problem of finding some stable relation among these three great elements of mankind lies at the root of all South African questions. It is, I suggest, the ultimate problem of the world.

The Dutch settlers, planted at Table Bay to raise vegetables for the Indian merchantmen, presently began to develop a view of their own not in harmony with that of the Company. To the Company in Holland, Cape Town was nothing but a stepping-stone to India.

To the Dutch settlers of the second generation, South Africa was their home. Moreover the sons of the Dutch gardeners and mechanics imported from Holland began to change their habits of life. As they multiplied they spread inland across the spit of sand which joins the Cape peninsula to the mainland. The Company thought of preventing any further connection with the interior by cutting the spit with a ditch and a wall, but nothing was done, and in course of years a tide of emigrants filtered across and settled the fertile lands which fringed the coast. At length they began to climb the Drakenstein Mountains to the high and arid table-land above, where the Karoo desert begins, a country suitable only for cattle. In that desolate region their habits continued to change. The original settlers were gardeners or sailors. Their descendants came to forget the arts of intensive culture. In a few generations the interior was covered by a sparse population of pastoralists whose home was largely the ox-wagon. To a great extent they reverted to the habits of their migratory ancestors who first invaded Europe from the East. Far beyond the reach of the feeble government in Cape Town, they repudiated its authority when any serious attempt was made to follow them. Before the end of the eighteenth century the authority of the Company was openly denied at Graaf Reinet.

In order to explain how England came on the scene we must glance again at the age of Queen Bess. English merchants had been content to allow the Dutch East India Company to divide the monopoly of the trade with the Portuguese. But in 1600 a sudden rise in the price of pepper led to the foundation of the British East India Company. For a century and a half this English company tried to confine itself to trade, avoiding political responsibilities in any shape or form. They refused to annex any harbor on the coast, contenting themselves with the Island of St. Helena as their half-way house. It was plain, however, that the power which held Cape Town held the key to the Eastern trade. In the course of the eighteenth century the struggle with France forced the British East India Company to abandon its purely commercial policy and to embark on the tasks of government in India. In 1795 France annexed Holland, just as Spain had previously annexed Portugal, and the British, who were then at war with France, seized Cape Town to prevent its falling into the hands of the French Government. They relinquished the place at the peace of Amiens, and took it back when that peace broke down. But when peace was finally made at Vienna in 1815, England purchased the Cape for six million pounds from the Netherlands.

Inspired by Wilberforce, the crusade for abolishing slavery was rapidly coming to a head. The sentiment behind it was largely the product of the Evangelical Movement. It involved a complete revolution in all the ideas which for three centuries had governed the relations of the white to the negro races. But it left the Boers in their remote wilderness untouched, and threw them into sharp antagonism with their new English rulers. In 1834 slavery in South Africa was abolished by act of the British Parliament. Two years later Lord Glenelg, the Colonial Secretary, who had been a strong supporter of the anti-slavery movement, ordered certain lands taken in one of the Kaffir wars and colonized by the Boers to be restored to the natives. In their indignation a large number of Boers resolved to retreat into the interior and place themselves beyond the reach of the Government. Crossing the Orange River, some of them settled in the country between that river and the Vaal, which is now the Orange Free State, with its capital at Bloemfontein. The more adventurous spirits overran the country north of the Vaal, and then, turning eastward, formed a republic at Pietermaritzburg in Natal, claiming jurisdiction down to the coast at Durban.

The British Government had no desire to possess South Africa for its own sake. Like the Dutch East India Company, they valued it only as the key to their Empire in India. Their aim, therefore, was to control the coast, but to avoid as far as possible responsibility for administering the interior, which would involve them in wars with the Kaffirs. In pursuit of this policy they refused to recognize the Boer Republic in Natal and brushed it back into the Transvaal. On the other hand they positively encouraged the creation in the hinterland of two independent republics. The upshot of this policy was the division of South Africa among three sovereignties. The coast country was divided between two colonies, both under the British flag, Cape Colony and Natal; while the interior was parceled out between the two republics of the Orange Free State and the Transvaal.

Sir George Grey, one of the greatest colonial governors ever sent out by England, was quick to see the mischief to which this policy would lead. He saw that South Africa was essentially one country with interests common to its people as a whole. A policy which aimed at separating the coast territories from those of the interior was contrary to the facts of nature. The inland republics were not really strong enough to deal with the powerful tribes of the interior, and their troubled relations with the natives would inevitably spread to the territories under British rule. He pointed out that if the whole white population could be united under one government responsible to the people of South Africa as a whole, that government would be strong enough to deal with native troubles, while the British Government could still prevent any foreign power from gaining a footing on the coast and threatening the safety of the route to India. Unfortunately all this ran counter to the doctrines of the Manchester School, which held that British interests were confined to trade and that the expansion of the Empire must be limited in every possible direction. The farsighted policy of Sir George Grey was vetoed in 1859, and an artificial disunion was definitely stamped on the map of South Africa.

Thucydides somewhere remarks that wars are occasioned by little things but caused by great ones. The South African war, like the late war, is a case in point. Most of you can remember the angry controversies of twenty years ago as to whether Rhodes, Chamberlain and Milner, or Kruger, Leyds, and Steyn were responsible for the outbreak of war. The real fact is that war was rendered inevitable when the counsels of Grey were ignored and partition was stamped on

South Africa in 1859. The causes which rendered that war inevitable were set in motion more than forty years before it broke out.

The essence of the whole situation was this: that the people of South Africa could never achieve the verities of responsible government so long as their country was divided under separate flags. I will try to explain why this was so.

To begin with, the inland republics were entirely dependent for their imports on goods introduced through the ports of Cape Colony and Natal. We have now come to a period when the governments of both these colonies were no longer controlled from England but were each responsible to a parliament and electorate of its own. In all domestic affairs their rights of self-government were just as complete as those of the inland republics. In a young community customs are really the main source of the public revenue. The inland republics justly claimed their right to the duties levied on the goods they consumed. That claim was denied by the parliaments of Cape Colony and Natal. The accidents of geography made it possible for the self-governing colonies on the coast to tax the people of the inland republics. A deep resentment in the minds of these people was the natural result. In the Cape parliament the majority were Dutch; but none the less the Boers in the two republics associated the injustice with British rule and turned their resentment against Great Britain.

In Canada today, if there is any question at issue between two or more parts of Canada or between two sections of the Canadian people, that question can be settled by a government responsible to the people of Canada as a whole. Whether the eastern provinces are at issue with the western, the Catholics with the Protestants, or the people of French with those of British descent, the British Government in England is never invoked to settle the quarrel. If Great Britain were constantly intervening in Canadian affairs, you can easily see how hateful her name would become to large sections of Canadians. When the Boer republics had been finally recognized there was then no power responsible to South Africans themselves which would settle their disputes with the Cape Colony or Natal. The consequence was that the British Government, located six thousand miles away, was constantly dragged in to settle these quarrels. Let me give you one case in point. The territories of the Transvaal, the Orange Free State, and the Cape Colony all converge near the point where the Vaal flows into the Orange River. The land in this region was so barren and worthless that neither of the three governments had taken the trouble to survey the boundaries. In the early seventies the richest diamond fields in the world were discovered in this No-Man's-Land, and each of the three governments hastened to claim the territory in which they lay. No data existed upon which a legal decision could be based. But a decision had to be made, and could only be made by the British Government, which settled the matter by paying £90,000 to the Orange Free State and annexing the diamond fields to Cape Colony. In the Boer republics the decision could scarcely fail to foster the growing feeling of resentment against the British flag.

A few years later the Transvaal, unable to collect customs on its imports, defaulted, and the value of its pound note fell to a shilling. Threatened with attack by a native tribe on its eastern borders, it was powerless to deal with the situation. For the moment a remedy was found by annexation to Great Britain. The government of the republic in its desperate position acquiesced. It was one thing, however, to proclaim annexation, and quite another to enforce it. Meanwhile, a Liberal government had replaced the Conservative government of Lord Beaconsfield, and Gladstone, who had always objected to annexation, came into power. In 1880 the burghers revolted and inflicted a signal defeat on the British forces at Majuba Hill. In 1881 Gladstone consented to the reëstablishment of the Transvaal Republic, which was significantly called the South African Republic. It was rapidly becoming clear that the problem would only find its solution in a union of the whole South African people. But such a union meant either that the British flag must be lowered in the two coast colonies, or else that the republican flags must be lowered in the Transvaal and the Orange Free State. That both flags had now been consecrated by blood was an added fact in the situation.

Five years later a discovery was made which was soon to turn this bankrupt state into the wealthiest in South Africa. Just as the richest diamond fields in the world had been discovered in Kimberley, so now in 1886 the gold fields of the Witwatersrand, the richest in the world, were discovered on the present site of Johannesburg—which took its name from my old friend Johannes Rissik, the surveyor-general of the Transvaal. In a few years these fields had attracted a mass of immigrants, or Uitlanders,* as the Boers called them, who were largely British. The population of the Transvaal was in fact doubled within the space of a few years. By the end of the century the Witwatersrand ridge was supporting a white population approximately equal to the whole of the Boer population in the rest of the Transvaal.

Obsessed by the not unnatural fear that this might lead to reannexation, the Boer population refused the uitlanders any right to share in the government of the country. Yet all but a negligible fraction of the public revenues was derived from their industry. Such a situation was bound to lead to a revolution which could scarcely fail to convulse the whole of South Africa. But no government was competent to handle the situation, because there was none responsible to the people of South Africa as a whole.

We must now turn for a moment to consider the results which had followed on the annexation of the Kimberley diamond mines to Cape Colony. A young Oxford man, Cecil Rhodes, had conceived the idea of using the wealth to be drawn from these mines as the means for a vast territorial development in the north. By a series of dexterous operations he succeeded in concentrating all the numerous diggings in one great corporation controlled by himself. Backed by the influence and fabulous wealth which he thus acquired, he presently became the Prime Minister of the Cape Colony. His first care had been to prevent the block-

* Pronounced "atelanders."

ing of his road to the north by the further extension of the Transvaal to the west.

The habits formed by the Boers centuries before, when they had first begun to move northward from the fertile coast into the wilderness, had remained unchanged. They had never relearned the methods of intensive agriculture, and as pastoralists they needed vast areas on which to feed their flocks. In the Transvaal the standard size of a Boer farm was seven thousand acres, and under its primitive constitution each burgher was entitled to two such farms, one in the low veldt for winter feeding, and another in the high veldt for the summer. The Boer population was still comparatively small, but the families multiplied quickly. It was common for a farmer to have ten children or more; and in these circumstances it was no wonder that all the available land between the Vaal and the Limpopo should have been appropriated well before the close of the nineteenth century. The old hereditary tendency of the younger children to take their share of the paternal flocks and trek further afield into the interior was as strong as ever. When the land available in the Transvaal had all been occupied the Boer population began to flow westward into Bechuanaland and northward across the Limpopo towards the interior of Central Africa. Rhodes saw the importance of keeping open that western road to the north. In 1884, while still a very young man, he managed to secure the dispatch of an expedition under Sir Charles Warren, which prevented the annexation of Bechuanaland by the Boers and compelled them to remain within their treaty frontier. The Transvaal

Republic was thus confined to the limits established by the Convention signed at Pretoria by which Gladstone had consented in 1881 to reëstablish the Republic. The road to the north was thus kept open. In 1888 Rhodes succeeded in making a treaty with Lobengula, the paramount chief north of the Limpopo, by which these territories were virtually brought under British protection. In 1889 he obtained a Royal Charter empowering the British South Africa Company, which he founded, to administer these territories, upon which Germany as well as the Transvaal was now casting a longing eye. There were thus brought under the British control new territories to the north of the Limpopo which in size are about equal to the whole area of the Cape Colony, Natal, the Free State, and the Transvaal added together.

To gain his objects Rhodes had not scrupled to use the power and prestige of the British Government in South Africa to the full. On the other hand, he realized more clearly than any one since Grey that nothing could go well with the country until it was included under one government responsible to the people of South Africa as a whole. But he found himself face to face with the inexorable factor of the separate sovereignties of the Boer Republic. "The key to the South African question," said Rhodes, "is to eliminate the Imperial factor." In plain words, the South African people must make themselves masters in their own house. They must establish a sovereignty responsible to themselves as a whole, instead of three or more severally responsible to separate sections of the South African people. But the three flags were fatal to union. Flags are the visible symbols of sovereignty, and real self-government could never be established until there was one flag recognized as supreme over all others. Either the British flag must disappear from Cape Colony, Natal, and Rhodesia, or else the republican flags must vanish from the Free State and the Transvaal. To an Englishman like Rhodes there could be only one alternative when faced by an issue like this. The shadow of German ambitions was already lengthening across the world. A united South Africa under a republican flag would certainly be drawn into her circle, and one of the great strategic positions of the world would pass from British to German control. The issues involved were by no means limited to South Africa herself.

Faced by this perilous dilemma Rhodes yielded to a temptation which time and time again has been the undoing of the greatest men—a passion to witness the accomplishment of his own dreams before he died. By 1895 he saw that the Transvaal was rushing headlong to revolution. Rhodes decided to get in touch with the revolutionaries and to mold the movement to his greater purpose. It was only at the last moment that he and his dashing lieutenant, Dr. Jameson, realized that the uitlander leaders were preoccupied with their own grievances, and had never given a thought to the larger project of South African union. Some forces of the South African Company had been collected under Dr. Jameson in Bechuanaland, just west of the Transvaal frontier, to be ready for contingencies. At the last moment Jameson realized that the uitlander leaders at Johannesburg had no intention of hoisting the British flag, but intended only to achieve control of the Transvaal for themselves under a republican flag. Jameson was one of those born leaders whom men will follow even when they think he is wrong. He was one of the humblest men I have ever known, but he knew by experience his own power of controlling a situation when once he was on the spot. He telegraphed to Rhodes that the only way to save a fiasco was for him and his force to cross the border and make his way to Johannesburg as quickly as possible. Rhodes saw the folly of the step and telegraphed back a peremptory refusal. I will now tell you what Jameson himself told me some fifteen years afterwards on an occasion which I shall describe to you later. On receiving the telegram he thought to himself: "Rhodes is the Prime Minister of the Cape, and of course as such he cannot make himself responsible for a proposal to invade the Transvaal Republic. It is up to me to take this responsibility on myself. And like a damned fool," he added, "I never saw that I could not do this thing without involving Rhodes himself."

It is needless to describe the fiasco which followed, a fiasco which brought not only South Africa but all Europe to the verge of war. An immediate catastrophe was averted by the moderation of President Kruger. The time had yet to come when he, like Rhodes, was destined to lose his grip on realities. He spared Jameson and the uitlander leaders from the scaffold to which they were justly condemned. But had General Botha then been in Kruger's place I have no doubt that he would have recognized the substantial justice of the uitlander demands, that he would have admitted them to the franchise and remedied their grievances. But even so I do not believe that war could have been long postponed. So long as South Africa remained divided under three separate flags the whole country was the victim of a subtle but creeping paralysis. Flags are not mere pieces of bunting. They are the visible symbols of the greatest fact in national life, the fact of sovereignty—of living realities which drive their roots with incredible swftness into the hearts of men. Once create them, and in a few years you cannot remove them without the tearing of flesh and the shedding of blood. The real lesson of South African history is that the division of one country under separate flags may render that country incapable of self-government until they are removed. You who have been careful to inscribe the stars of all your states on one flag may recognize the virtue of applying that principle to countries other than your own.

To remove this obstacle to union and to enable the people of South Africa to manage their own affairs without the need or chance of interference from Great Britain was the real achievement of the South African war. One cannot help thinking now how incredulous we who were fighting out there would have been had any one told us this at the time. Yet, looking back, nothing is clearer in the light of after events.

But while the war made the union possible, it did not accomplish the union itself. Indeed the war was scarcely over before the old symptoms of disunion began to reassert themselves in all their multifarious forms. The fact is all the more significant because the governments throughout South Africa were all of British complexion. To begin with, the Transvaal and Orange Free State were organized as Crown colonies under the control of the British High Commissioner, Lord Milner, who after a few years was succeeded by Lord Selborne. Natal was British as always, while in the Cape Colony the disfranchisement of the Dutch rebels had placed in power a British Government with Dr. Jameson at its head. I knew most of the ministers who composed these governments and actually lived with some of them in the Transvaal, and I am bound to say that they impressed me as disinterested men with an exceptionally high standard of honor. But one could not fail also to be impressed with the fact that as time went on each of these four governments came to conceive a worse opinion and to be more distrustful of the other three. One could not but feel that there must be something radically vicious in a system which caused perfectly honorable men to think so ill of each other. In truth, it was a system under which no really important question could ever be brought to a final and conclusive decision. I will try to illustrate this from some of the more important departments of public administration, and explain the consequent reactions on business conditions.

Before the war the Cape Colony, Natal, the Transvaal Republic, and the Orange Free State each had power to frame a separate tariff of its own, and exercised that power. And what is more, each of their legislatures had power to change their tariff every year, and frequently did so. As usually happens in a new country, these tariffs were frankly protective.

They were meant to encourage the establishment of productive industries in the country itself. But no one of the four communities was large enough in itself to provide a market sufficient to support a productive industry of any importance. Industries worth having could only be created with a view to the market of South Africa taken as a whole. Business men who had not studied the political conditions or realized how essentially unstable they were, would take note of the existing tariffs throughout the country. They would make their calculations on the basis of those tariffs and arrive at the conclusion that a profitable industry could be started. It was not one tariff which they had to consider, but four, each of which was subject to yearly change. They would build a factory and equip it with machinery and begin to produce, only to find that in the meantime one or more of the separate legislatures had changed its tariff and falsified the whole of their calculations.

The evils were so flagrant that after the war every one was agreed that a remedy must be found. The obvious remedy was political union. But every one agreed to think of political union as something which must be accomplished sooner or later, but certainly not before the time of their grandchildren. As I have tried to show you here, the divisions of South Africa were the result of a long series of accidents and mistakes. But almost every one seemed to cling to them as if they were divinely ordained. Really, you have to live in a new country to realize what a terrific force in human nature conservatism is, and how intensely people will cling to thoroughly bad arrangements if once they rank as established institutions. Every one tried by tinkering with details to mend a system which was wrong in principle. In the hope of avoiding union a number of counterfeit substitutes were tried.

After the war every one was agreed that there must be one tariff for the whole country. So delegates from all the four colonies met under the presidency of Lord Milner. In the Transvaal the interests of the gold-mining industry demanded low costs of production, and therefore a low tariff on imports. The interests of the Cape Colony and Natal were the very opposite. Their business consisted largely in raising produce for the Transvaal, and their interests consequently lay in the direction of high tariffs. However, under the spell of Lord Milner's paramount influence, a compromise was arrived at, and the delegates from the four colonies succeeded in framing a tariff which each of them undertook to recommend for adoption to their several legislatures. This had all to be done in the strictest secrecy to prevent speculation on the markets. The numerous interests affected by the tariff had thus no chance of expressing their views until it was published. Your tariff, of course, is framed in the secrecy of the executive government; but before it becomes law it goes to Congress, just as ours goes to Parliament, and in our legislatures the various interests which are pinched or hurt by the tariff can make their voices heard. Changes can be made, and are freely made, by the legislature as a result. But in order to take effect the customs convention in South Africa had to be ratified not by one legislature but by four. And each of the legislatures had to be warned that if they exercised their constitutional right to amend a single item in the schedule the whole customs convention would almost certainly be wrecked. They had to take or leave the schedule just as it was. They might discuss it, but they must not alter a single word of it. In plain words, each of the four legislatures had to abandon the right to control the tariff and leave the right to the exclusive control of the executive. Such was the influence of Lord Milner that for once the legislatures acquiesced and agreed to abandon their legitimate functions. The convention was thoroughly unpopular from the outset. Every one knew it must break down and no one was prepared to invest his capital on the strength of it. The realities of popular control were in fact destroyed by the artificial divisions of the country.

The convention operated to sow distrust between the four communities and their several governments. Let me illustrate this by a single instance. The customs revenue was collected at the ports, but had to be divided among the four governments in proportion to the amount of goods consumed in each colony. By an elaborate and expensive machinery, which was highly vexatious in its operation, the ultimate destination of the goods had then to be traced in order that the revenue levied upon them at the port might be duly credited to the colony in which the goods were actually consumed. Now to meet the wishes of Natal, the only part of South Africa in which sugar was produced, the Transvaal had reluctantly agreed to a swinging duty on sugar. All the same Natal was unable to produce sugar enough for the needs of the whole country. After the customs convention had been in operation for a few years an extraordinary phenomenon was observed. The whole of the sugar consumed in Natal was imported from her chief competitor Mauritius. The enormous duties levied on this imported sugar were, under the convention, credited to Natal. On the other hand all the sugar produced in the plantations of Natal was forwarded for consumption in the Transvaal. But as there was no duty on sugar produced in South Africa the Transvaal got no duties on the Natal sugar it consumed. For some time the Transvaal Government was unable to explain this phenomenon, till suddenly it was discovered that the government of Natal, which controlled the railways of Natal, had granted a special low rate for the carriage of sugar produced in the country. It came to light that the Cape Colony had also been using its control of freights to protect the produce of its own farmers. You can readily understand the indignation aroused in the Transvaal by discoveries like these, and how it was that the various governments became so distrustful of each other.

The wealth of the Transvaal had made her the dominant power in South Africa, and in consequence she was viewed with an ever-growing dislike by the coast colonies. The discovery of the gold fields in 1886 had in fact turned the tables. Before the gold fields were discovered the coast colonies had been able to levy taxation for their own benefit on the imports of the Transvaal and the Orange Free State. After 1886 the equipment of the mines must have cost little short of £100,000,000, and involved a vast importation of goods from the coast. In order to reap the benefits of this carrying trade the Cape Colony and Natal both spent vast sums of money on equipping their ports and building railways to the Transvaal border. A glance at the map will show you that the traffic from these colonies passed over only relatively short sections within the territory of the Transvaal itself. The consequence of this was that only a small proportion of the profits in the carrying trade accrued to the benefit of the Transvaal revenues. But a glance at the map will also show you that goods introduced through the port of Delagoa Bay in Portuguese territory, would reach Johannesburg by a much shorter route, running for all but the first fifty miles through Transvaal territory, so that all but a small fraction of the profits on transit would accrue to the Transvaal. President Kruger was quick to see his advantage and pressed forward the construction of a line from Pretoria to Delagoa Bay. The opening of this line shortly after the Jameson Raid soon began to turn the profits which the Cape and Natal had reaped from the carrying trade into a loss. The inevitable crisis was delayed by the war, which lasted for close on three years. But as soon as peace was declared and normal conditions began to prevail, Lord Milner found himself in the shoes of President Kruger. If traffic were allowed by the government of the Transvaal to take its normal course, the traffic would increasingly pass to Delagoa Bay, and immense profits would be reaped by the Transvaal, while the British ports and railways of the Cape and Natal would drift rapidly towards bankruptcy. The result was a compromise. Lord Milner agreed with the coast colonies to fix the rates in such a way that a certain amount of traffic would still be secured to them. This of course involved a sacrifice of revenue to the Transvaal which its people viewed with the deepest resentment, so that it was perfectly clear that Lord Milner would not be sustained if he were responsible to a Transvaal electorate. A feeling that they lay at the mercy of the Transvaal was the source of a resentment no less bitter in the coast colonies.

Customs and railways were the two immediate factors which drove South Africa to union, because the consequences of disunion in these branches of administration were felt so acutely in the daily life of the people. But to thoughtful and observant minds it was plain that an even greater danger was impending. As already remarked, the relation of the European, Asiatic, and Negro populations is the question fundamental to all others in South Africa. Since the early importation of Malay slaves the Cape and also the Orange Free State had avoided any further importation of Asiatic labor. Natal, on the other hand, had embarked on the policy of founding her industries on labor imported from India. In that colony the Asiatic population presently exceeded the white. The Transvaal after the war, by importing indentured laborers from China, had taken a dangerous step in the same direction. With regard to the native population the North and the South were traveling fast in diametrically opposite directions. The policy which had inspired the abolition of slavery had under the influence of governors like Grey taken deep root in the Cape Colony.

The policy was afterwards crystallized by Rhodes in the formula "Equal rights to all civilized men." In pursuance of this principle the right to vote had been accorded to educated natives, and large sums of public money were annually spent on native education.

The great trek which had led to the foundation of republics north of the Orange River and the Vaal was in fact set in motion by a spirit of revolt against this policy. It is significant that both republics inserted the following article in their Grondwets or constitutions: "In church and state there is no equality between black and white." In pursuance of this principle the right to vote was never accorded to natives in the Transvaal and Free State, and practically nothing was spent, except by the missionaries, on their education. In this matter the gulf which divided the Cape Colony from the rest of South Africa was as wide and difficult to bridge as the gulf which divided the northern states of the American Union from the South up to the time of the great civil war.

The conflicts of policy were so serious that Lord Milner persuaded the four colonies to appoint a joint commission to examine the native question throughout South Africa. It produced a unanimous report in favor of the policy of the Cape, and made a number of practical recommendations. But the separate colonies made no serious attempt to carry these recommendations into effect. Rather the cleavage of opinion grew wider every day. It was clear to all thoughtful minds that one policy for the whole country must be the product of one electorate and not of four.

We must now return to trace the course of events.

The introduction of Chinese labor had led to a profound revulsion of feeling in England. The Conservative government resigned, and in 1906 Campbell-Bannerman was returned to power by an overwhelming majority. He lost no time in announcing his intention to confer full responsible government on the Transvaal and Orange Free State. British officials in the Crown Colony government who had watched the situation closely knew that this was the only possible course. But while they recognized its wisdom they were more alive to its dangers than ministers in England. For the last five years equilibrium had only been maintained by the great authority of the two beneficent despots who had ruled the inland colonies, Lord Milner and his successor, Lord Selborne. In the field of railway and customs administration they, as rulers of the Transvaal, had maintained equilibrium by making concessions to the interests of Cape Colony and Natal which no government removable by voters in the Transvaal could possibly sustain. It was evident that their policy was impossible for ministers responsible to a Transvaal electorate. So long as South Africa remained divided into four communities the inland colonies stood to gain by denouncing the various conventions which regulated customs and rates. The coast colonies would then rapidly drift into bankruptcy and a general confusion ensue which would easily develop into war.

It must not, however, be supposed that in 1906 they saw the problem or its solution as I have stated it today. For six years they had been too deeply engaged on the everyday tasks of administration to study the history of South Africa. They had stood too near the canvas to see the outlines, but from their own limited experience they knew that the grant of self-government to the two former republics would be the prelude to a new and perhaps disastrous crisis in the old South African problem. They asked themselves what they could do to solve the problem, and so found themselves asking what the problem itself was. Before undertaking to suggest a remedy it seemed more reasonable to try to arrive at a diagnosis. So, while the preparations for establishing responsible government were in train, they began to study South African history in the light of their own recent experience and to visit the other colonies for the purpose. The conclusions at which they arrived were those which I have tried to present to you to-night. The South African question did not arise from a conflict of races, the British and Boer, as every one with the war so fresh in his memory was inclined to assume. The root of the trouble lay not in the conflict of races, but in the conflict of states. A country and people designed by nature to be organized into one state had been parcelled out as a number of different states. There was no paramount authority responsible to the people as a whole. There was no one organ through which the people of the country could conceive and execute policies for the country as a whole. The only remedy was for the people of South Africa to establish one government responsible to themselves and competent to decide any question at issue between two or more of its separate communities. A correct diagnosis of a disease points to its remedy.

It was one thing, however, to see the remedy and quite another to get it adopted. An experience of autocratic government is apt to give those who work under it a great distrust of public opinion. For six years they had only had to persuade one strong, intelligent, and highly disinterested ruler that this or that reform was needed; and then it had often to be carried out in the teeth of public opinion. Now they were on the eve of a change after which nothing could be done until public opinion had first been convinced that it had to be done. But believing as they did that existing conditions, if left to drift, would end in a renewal of war, their only alternative was to attempt the seemingly hopeless task of converting public opinion. So they published their case. The results were a revelation. They discovered for themselves the truth, that men with a real case who will state it fairly and argue it patiently can count in the end on convincing public opinion.

Lord Bryce pointed out last year that historical events are not the result of mere physical forces. The personal element may change the whole situation. That was certainly true of South Africa. I believe that the Union could not have been carried in time to avoid a catastrophe but for the presence of four men, General Smuts, Lord Selborne, Dr. Jameson, and General Botha. Union could never have been carried without the assent of the British in South Africa. It meant, and we all knew that it meant, placing the British for the rest of our lives, not only in the Free State and the Transvaal, but also in Natal and the

Cape Colony, under the rule of the Boer generals whom we had fought in the war. I need scarcely remind you that one of them, with the earnest support of the British, is ruling South Africa today. I do not believe that the British could ever have been brought to support the movement if Lord Selborne had not taken the lead from the outset, and if Dr. Jameson had not thrown his whole influence into the scale in favor of the Union. I shall never forget one evening when I had come down from the Transvaal with Herbert Baker, the great architect who is now building the capitol at Delhi and the Bank of England, to persuade Dr. Jameson to take this step. We stayed with him at Groote Schuur, the wonderful house which Baker had built for Rhodes, and which was left by him as a future residence for the Prime Minister of the Union he was never destined to see. We urged our case as best we could. We told Jameson that he alone of all our leaders could persuade the British to take this step. Jameson was silent and hung back. Suddenly—I can see him now—he pushed back his chair from the table, looked us straight in the face, and said: "Don't forget that the man you are asking to try this is the man who has committed the greatest crime in South Africa." Then for two hours this usually reticent man unpacked his heart and told us the inner history of the raid. I have never listened to so terrible and convincing an indictment of a man by himself. One agreed with that indictment and felt none the less that the man who could tell this story of himself was one of the noblest who had ever lived. He ended by doing what we asked, and I always felt that the work he did for the South African Union was an offering of atonement.

It was in this task that Jameson and Botha formed for each other an attachment which was not surprising to those who know how great and how lovable both men were. And yet what other case can history show of two leaders not merely of opposite parties, but of two races, who loved each other like David and Jonathan? The greatness of Botha—and he was the greatest man I ever met or am ever likely to meet—was shown by his recognition of the fact that union could be carried only by the free consent of the British minority. Often during the Irish crisis I have said to myself: "Oh, for one hour of Botha!"

The dream of Rhodes will not be completed until the vast territories which bear his name are included in the Union. In those regions is a lofty summit, strewn with boulders huge and erratic like himself, where Rhodes loved to sit and brood. It is a great and solemn place. He named it "The World's View," and left it as a national place of burial for those who had deserved well of their country. There he rests, and Jameson with him. I sometimes dream that when Rhodesia enters the Union, Botha, the greatest of all the South Africans, may be brought to rest by his peers on that lonely and wind-swept height of the Matoppos.

LECTURE II

Responsible Government in India

FROM the story I have told you two thoughts emerge. I will ask you to keep them in mind while you listen to still another story.

First—the paramount importance of time: Suppose that the Union had not been carried in 1909—suppose that South Africa had remained with all its divisions unhealed till 1914—and then consider the results. In the general upheaval of the great war, a civil conflict would have broken out into which England would most certainly have been drawn. As it was, the rebellion of Beyers was a mere flash in the pan, easily suppressed by the Union Government, and nearly the whole force of South Africa was then thrown on the side of the Allies. In a balance so evenly weighted a relatively small factor may turn the scale. The timely union of South Africa modified the results of that mighty struggle and may even have determined its issue. To render fireproof inflammable structures which are liable to be lit by sparks from outside, or which may, if fired from within, spread their flames to the whole fabric of human society, is the surest way of preventing, limiting, or abbreviating war.

The second thought I am trying to suggest is this: In the long run no measures will render such dangerous structures safe which are not calculated to realize the verities of responsible government. This brings me to the subject of my second lecture.

I have previously mentioned that the British East India Company was incorporated in the year 1600. At that time the greater part of India was organized under the strong and enlightened rule of Akbar, the greatest of the Mogul emperors. Mogul, a version of our word Mongol, was a misnomer applied to the northern conquerors of India in much the same way as the Germans were called Huns by their enemies in the Great War. Akbar's grandfather Baba, who was known as the Tiger, was the chieftain of a vigorous white race in central Asia, not improbably of Aryan stock like ourselves, but Mohammedan by religion. Baba was a man of titanic strength and energy. By a series of conquests he, his son, and his grandson Akbar, had consolidated the kingdoms of Northern India into the so-called Mogul Empire. The vast majority of the people of that country were of course Hindu by religion. A certain number had been converted to Islam by the sword, so that there are in India to-day nearly 70,000,000 Mohammedans as against some 220,-000,000 Hindus.

The Mogul Empire was the nearest approach to a just and orderly government which India had seen before the days of British rule. The heads of these kingdoms were largely replaced by hereditary satraps ruling vast provinces under the Emperor's authority.

I may here draw your attention to a fact of which I shall have more to say later on. There is in self-governing communities an unconscious tendency to split up and keep themselves small. The growth of commonwealths has involved a conscious effort to overcome this fissiparous habit. Autocracies, on the other hand, lend themselves to the development of large areas. The vast size of the provinces inherited by British India from the Mogul Empire is today a real impediment to the growth of self-government in India.

The government of Akbar and of his immediate successors was at least efficient, and the Company found themselves trading in a civilized country where substantial order was maintained. They asked and obtained leave to establish warehouses* on the coast, where Indian merchandise could be collected for shipment to England. To begin with, these warehouses were perfectly safe. But in the course of the next century and a half the emperors grew weak. The great satraps increasingly ignored their authority and quarreled among themselves. The country relapsed into general disorder, and to protect their property the Company was obliged to fortify the warehouses where their merchandise was collected at the ports. It was thus that the great modern cities of Bombay, Madras, and Calcutta were brought into existence. Unlike great inland cities, such as Agra, Delhi, and Allahabad, these coast towns were from the first the creations of British enterprise. The nucleus of each of them today is the fort surrounding the warehouses of the old East India Company.

* These establishments were always called factories, but I am going to call them warehouses, because that expresses in modern language what they really were.

The world-wide struggle between France and England was the keynote of the eighteenth century. It was in essence a conflict between the principle of the commonwealth and that of autocracy. The existence of free institutions in America today is due to its issue. Readers of Admiral Mahan's works will remember his account of the resentment felt in New England when the colonists had undertaken and accomplished the taking of Louisburg, and at the end of the Seven Years' War Louisburg was handed back to the French in exchange for Madras, which had been taken by the French from the English. I, who have lived in new countries, can well realize the indignation which was felt in this country. But Admiral Mahan, as you will remember, devotes several pages to showing that this exchange was in principle right and sound. I refer to the matter only to show you how very closely connected the history of India in the eighteenth century was with the development of free institutions in this country. It was purely a question of sea power, and the revenues which either protagonist could derive from the Indian trade affected the relative strength of their fleets. In India France was also represented by a trading company, and when England and France were at war the two companies in India were naturally in conflict. Clive and Dupleix were the rival leaders in the Seven Years' War. Dupleix' policy was to enlist the support of great Indian satraps by helping them in their quarrels against other Indian potentates. The natural result was that those other potentates enlisted the help of the British. The French and British troops engaged were mere handfuls. They were only the backbone of much larger native forces which as time went on were brought more and more under the direction of the French and English generals.

In the theory of Indian government the ruler is entitled to all the produce of the land not required for the actual support of the cultivator. If the ruler tried to collect too much, the cultivator fled to the jungle, and an inexorable limit was thus set to the share in the produce which the ruler could collect. Akbar's greatest reform consisted in fixing the amount due to the state at one-fourth of the gross produce, and also in making a cadastral survey. If you go to the remotest village in central India you will find a complete plan of every field surrounding the village, kept up to date by the village patwari, with an estimate of the revenue due from that field. On the basis of this survey, the amount due from each holding was fixed for five years. The element of certainty thus created was an immense boon to the Indian peasant and explains the comparative prosperity which followed the rule of Akbar. Of course these revenues were not collected directly by the Emperor; they were collected by the nawab or satrap, who handed over a proportion to the Emperor, retaining the rest for the expenses of the Province and of his own establishment. The right to collect these revenues is the prize for which Indian conquerors have always contested. Indian potentates were in the habit of assigning the right to collect revenues from a certain area—a right called a jaghir—as the reward for those who had served them.

It was, as you know, in the struggle for the mastery

of Bengal, the vast estuary irrigated by the waters of the Ganges, that Clive beat the French and their allies. The nawab with whom Clive was allied rewarded his victories by a grant of the revenues of Bengal, Behar, and Orissa. Clive and his friends kept a share of the plunder for themselves, wondering, as he afterwards said to a parliamentary committee, at his own moderation. But the bulk of these revenues became the property of the Company. Before this the Company had earned its dividends from the profits of trade. They now began to depend largely on the revenues collected from Indian peasants.

The corruption by which the conquerors were enriched began to react on British politics. It was the age of rotten boroughs, which, as you know, were freely bought and sold. They ranked in English law as real property. Clive owned quite a large number of seats in Parliament, the members for which were his nominees. It was this which first drew the attention of Parliament to the state of affairs in India, and led to the appointment of a long series of parliamentary committees and debates in the House of Commons. It was in the course of these inquiries and debates that British public opinion came to realize the iniquity of existing conditions in India. The public conscience was aroused by the eloquence of men like Edmund Burke. Thus the idea gradually developed that the European had no right to make his own enrichment the motive of his government in India. English society began to conceive the principle that India ought to be governed with an eye to the welfare of its own people. The motives by which men are inspired are strangely mixed. Clive, in spite of his personal corruption, himself became a zealot in the cause of reform, and, strange as it may seem, was the first British ruler in India to organize these reforms under Parliamentary authority. His policy consisted in reviving and extending the principles of revenue initiated by Akbar. The cadastral survey was brought up to date, and the proportion of produce collected by the Company, to which the government was entrusted, was fixed for considerable periods and over large areas once for all. It was fixed much lower than Akbar fixed it, and has since the days of Clive been steadily reduced by the British Government.

Now comes one of the most interesting transitions in the history of British administration in India. This system of collecting revenue was quickly developed into a machinery for administering justice, for maintaining order, and generally for promoting the welfare of the people. In other words, intelligent administrators soon discovered that in order to collect the greatest amount of revenue you had to establish a just and orderly government. All this was done with such success that British authority rapidly extended over India. The native satraps were everywhere collapsing by reason of the corrupt and oppressive nature of the system by which they ruled, so that the mass of the people were glad to accept British authority. It is of importance to add that the growth of corruption in native states here, as in other parts of Asia and Africa, was aggravated by the presence of European adventurers in search of wealth. In order to control these adventurers the British Government was constantly impelled to intervene in the affairs of native states and, in many cases, to assume responsibility for their administration. It was mainly in this way that two-thirds of India was incorporated in provinces under the direct control of British administrators. In the other third, some hundreds of native princes were recognized as independent rulers but subject to treaties and to British supervision, under which the people were to some extent protected from oppression. It is important to remember that one-third of the great Indian peninsula remains today under the direct authority of native princes. All this of course involved a series of wars, and the conquests were effected by large Indian forces to some extent led by British officers and usually backed by British troops.

I cannot here enter into the complicated relations between the East India Company and the British Government, but from the days of Clive onwards the governor-general was practically appointed by the British Government. From 1848 to 1856 this office was filled by Lord Dalhousie, one of the ablest and most vigorous rulers that Britain has ever sent out. This period, you will observe, was just when Europe and America were beginning to realize the importance of mechanical forces as applied to transportation and communication. Dalhousie labored with extraordinary ability at the task of equipping this vast population with all the appliances of a modern civilized state. He constructed canals, railways, and roads, and covered the country with a network of telegraphs. The ideas of the people were scarcely beyond the stage reached by Europe in the early Middle Ages. Suppose for a moment that in the course of the Dark Ages China had discovered how to apply science to the things of daily life, and suppose also that China had conquered Europe in the days of the Plantagenets and had in a few years equipped it with railways and telegraphs—you can picture to yourselves the profoundly disruptive effects of changes so sudden on the civilization of the Middle Ages. It was just such a pouring of new wine into old bottles that Dalhousie accomplished in India. The mere disturbance effected by expropriating rights of way for railways was profound. If you read the history of the Indian mutiny which broke out the year after Dalhousie left India in 1857, you will find obscure and ingenious explanations of its causes, such as the grease used on cartridges. The pious Hindu views the eating of the flesh of cows with as great abhorrence as you and I would view the eating of human flesh. The rumor spread about that in order to destroy their caste the British Government was putting grease on the cartridges of the Sepoy Hindu soldiers in the British army. In those days the cartridge was just a measure of powder. The soldier bit off the end and poured the powder into the musket. This is often assigned as the main cause of the Indian mutiny. Well, a match thrown by an incendiary after a drought may perhaps be described as the cause of a forest fire. As I said in my last lecture, wars are occasioned by small things and caused by great ones. The real cause of the Indian mutiny was the sudden imposition of organized modern equipment on a people whose ideas were still those of an age centuries before such equipment was thought of.

The mutiny was followed by two important results.

(1) The survival of the Company involved a certain dualism in the system of Indian government, which naturally led to difficulties. Government through a chartered company has this inherent defect: that its directors are divided in mind whether to think first of the welfare of the people or the dividends of their shareholders. After the mutiny, the Company was finally abolished, and the government of India was made directly responsible through a secretary of state to the British Parliament.

(2) The second step was of even greater importance. In a proclamation issued in the name of Queen Victoria, the actuating principle of the British Government in India was expressly defined as the welfare of the natives of India themselves. Such declarations are not deprived of their importance by inevitable failures to realize them fully. Like the Ten Commandments, the Beatitudes, the declaration of the Allies during the war in favor of self-determination, or the "fourteen points" of President Wilson, they established a standard by which conduct can at any rate be gauged.

I will now endeavor to draw for you the outline of the British political system in India. It was mainly determined by previous conditions. The Company, I should have said, had always governed in the name of the Mogul emperor. The last Mogul emperor was dethroned in the mutiny. In the new system, the viceroy, advised by his executive council, took the place of the Mogul emperor, but the heads of the various provinces were governors who took the place of the nawabs or satraps who had ruled under the Moguls. Leaving aside minor areas, there are nine of these provinces: Bengal, Bombay, Madras, Behar and Orissa, the United Provinces of Agra and Oudh, the Punjab, Burma, the Central Provinces, and Assam. The United Provinces is the largest of the satrapies. For the purposes of discussion I will take it as a type. Its population is upwards of forty-eight millions—more than that of the whole British Isles. It is parceled out into forty-eight districts which correspond more or less to British or American counties, and in each of these there is on the average a million people. At the head of each is the district officer, commonly called the collector. He has little or nothing to do with the collection of revenue, but the name survives from the early days when Clive appointed British officials to collect the revenues. Under a reformed system their judicial and administrative functions grew far more important than their work of collecting revenue. The district officer took his orders from the governor of the province, and the governor took his orders from the governor-general. The governor enacted laws for each province, the governor-general and his council enacted laws for the whole of British India.

It was, to start with, the machinery of a pure autocracy, but with this difference: that the governor-general was responsible to Parliament in England, the autocracy was controlled by a commonwealth, and gradually the ideas of a commonwealth came to be imposed on the autocratic machinery. The rule of law, the idea that all government is to be conducted in accordance with written statutes, is essential to the commonwealth. So, from the outset of British rule, the lines within which the government might act were prescribed in the form of statutes framed by the governor-general and his council, a body of about half a dozen men. That was for India as a whole. Under the British constitution, all important laws are drafted by the executive whose duty it will be to administer them. In England the draft then comes before Parliament, the representatives of the people who are to obey the law, and they can amend it to any extent they like. It always happens that Parliament sees points in which the law may bear hardly on this or that interest, and amends the draft accordingly. In the first place, members of Parliament are criticizing something which is not their own creation. In the second place, they are viewing the draft from the point of view of those who will have to obey the law and not merely from the point of view of those who have to enforce it. In the early days of the Crown Colony government of the Transvaal I was able to watch the results of laws being made by an executive and promulgated without reference to any larger body. Apart from the question of popular government, I have realized ever since how important it is to the executive itself that measures should be submitted to the criticism of entirely fresh minds before they pass into law. Now Dalhousie, though he was a great autocrat, was also a parliamentarian, and he felt this in India. He was horrified to find that laws were drafted by the half dozen members of the executive council. Then, having settled the draft, they declared themselves to be the legislative council and went through the motions of a legislature in a few minutes. To cure this evil, Dalhousie appointed some additional members to the legislative council, so that when the executive council resolved itself into a legislature other prominent persons who had not yet seen the Bill walked in, and the Bill, before it became law, was thus exposed to the criticism of fresh minds.

The duty of the state to prepare its citizens to take part in its public affairs is a natural corollary to the principle of the commonwealth. The instincts of a despotism are always against education. Public affairs are not considered as the business of its subjects, and a despotism does not wish to help them to the knowledge which will enable them to criticize its acts. There are plenty of exceptions either way, but I am speaking of general tendencies, the force of which is beyond question. Now public opinion in England demanded the extension of education to India from the beginning of the nineteenth century. A great attempt was made, by those who feared the introduction of western ideas, to restrict this education to oriental studies. The attempt was defeated by Lord Macaulay, who was then a member of the viceroy's executive council. It was due to his influence that western literature was made the basis of instruction in the schools and colleges established by the British Government in India. The great masterpieces of English literature, like Milton's Areopagitica and Mill's works on Liberty and Self-Government, became the textbooks of Indian students. Hence the steady growth of an educated class which demanded the application of those principles to the polity of India. About forty years ago a body called the Indian National Congress, which met every year, was organized to voice these claims. They first demanded that some of the additional members appointed to the Indian legislative council should be Indians. When this was conceded, they began to ask that these Indians should be elected, and that Indian members should be appointed to the executive as well as to the legislative council. They also claimed that all these reforms should be applied to the governments of the various provinces.

I have not time to trace in detail the steps by which these demands were conceded. In 1880 Lord Ripon tried to inaugurate the principle of representation in district and municipal councils, that is to say, in the sphere of local administration. Of this I shall have more to say in my next lecture. The great era of political reform was opened when Morley became Secretary of State for India in 1906. Indian members were included by him in the various executive councils, and in 1909 a Bill was passed through the British Parliament at his instance, providing for the election of a minority of members in all the legislative councils. The executive was to remain responsible to the British Parliament in England, and its authority in the legislatures was to be secured by the appointment of a majority of the members, who could only speak and vote subject to the direction of the executive.

To judge from contemporary records, one gathers that Morley, Lord Minto, the Viceroy, and his advisers seemed to think that these reforms were final. Indians could now make their voices heard on all public questions. That a time must come when Indians themselves must decide those questions was a notion they never seemed to have grasped. Indeed, to entertain such an idea was regarded even by liberal statesmen as the mark of an incorrigible dreamer. British public opinion was convinced of its own permanent duty to provide good government for India. The belief that Indians could not provide nearly so good a government for themselves was accepted as a final argument against any ultimate transfer of responsibility to Indian hands. The fact that Indians could now make their voices heard was regarded as an effective guaranty against any risk of misgovernment. It was felt, in a word, that full effect had been given the pledges made in the great proclamation of Queen Victoria after the mutiny. It had scarcely crossed the public mind that Indians might have an interest greater even than a pure and efficient administration.

There is nothing an Englishman hates so much as to think in general terms, or to theorize. To enunciate principles he still feels is a trifle "French." But the outbreak of the war surprised us into formulating the principles for which we were fighting. There were real issues at stake. In unconscious obedience to the principle of autocracy which inspired their institutions, the Germans claimed to settle the destiny of the world. The nations they attacked resisted their claim, and asserted the right of nations to shape their destinies for themselves. This claim, championed by England, could not be denied to India, loyally fighting at her side. On the 20th of August, 1917, a solemn pronouncement in Parliament was made by Mr. Montagu,

Secretary of State for India, in which England recognized not representative but responsible government as the goal of her policy in India. Indians were to decide Indian questions for themselves as soon as they could be brought into a position to do so, and everything possible was to be done to help them to that position. The question remained, What practical steps were to be taken in this direction?

A plan was put forward by the Indian National Congress at their session at Lucknow in the last days of 1916, at which I happened to be present. The Indian National Congress was mainly a Hindu organization. The other great religion was represented politically by the All-India Moslem League. The League met at Lucknow at the same time as the Congress, and both parties agreed upon the same scheme of reforms, which was afterwards known as the Congress-League scheme. It was as great an achievement as if the Orangemen and the Nationalist Party in Ireland had met and agreed on a scheme of home rule. Under this scheme the executives were to become largely Indian, and an overwhelming majority of Indians were to be elected to the legislatures: and these reforms were to apply to the government of India as well as to the governments of the nine provinces. The same principles inspired the milder proposals put forward by the government of India. Under both these schemes majorities elected by Indian electorates were to have complete control of legislation and supply. The executives, on the other hand, though largely Indianized, were to remain responsible to Parliament in England, through the Secretary of State.

That is to say, they were appointed and could only be dismissed by the Secretary of State. The adverse vote of the legislature could not remove them from office, as in England or Canada. You must realize that this was the system which Indian opinion was demanding in 1917, and which British opinion was prepared to concede. And yet I do not hesitate to say that it was a system which has once disrupted the British Commonwealth and, in spite of repeated warnings, has again and again threatened it with disruption.

In order to explain this remark I must ask you to recall the process by which the absolute autocrats who ruled England from William the Conqueror to Edward I were gradually transformed into the hereditary President in whose name the government of the British Commonwealth is now conducted. The first Parliament was summoned by Edward I. By the time of the Stuarts it had acquired an exclusive right to control all legislation, including the levying of taxes and the grant of supplies. The functions of the king were limited to administering the laws made by Parliament and to spending revenues placed at his disposal on lines which Parliament prescribed. The difficulty was that the King and Parliament viewed the tasks of government from different angles, and were always at odds with one another. Charles I tried to dispense with Parliament, and the quarrel ended by Parliament dispensing with Charles I. Harmony between the executive and legislature could be secured only at the cost of a revolution. The defect of the whole system was that leaders like Hampden and Pym who guided Parliament in the making of laws and control of the revenues had no final responsibility for the results which followed. The tasks of defending the country and enforcing the law did not fall upon them, so that they did not realize, as a responsible executive only can realize, the difficulties and dangers involved in the restrictions which Parliament imposed. The restoration of Charles II was followed by a number of makeshifts, until the situation was relieved by the accession to the throne of two German princes, George I and George II, who were more interested in their German territories than in England and did not understand the English language. In their reigns the leaders of Parliament as ministers of the King became the real executive, governing in the King's name. The problem was solved by the fact that ministers could dissolve Parliament and appeal to the electorate, and if the verdict of the electorate was against them, they could then resign and their place was taken by the leaders of the new Parliamentary majority. Ministers, moreover, could resign if a majority in Parliament tried to impose impossible conditions or refused to vote money which was needed for the proper conduct of government. The leaders of the opposition were always restrained by the knowledge that they might themselves be called upon to conduct the government. Under this system the King was relegated to much the same position as the President now holds in the French Republic.

George III, who unfortunately spoke English, refused to accept this principle, and reverted to the old system. The American Revolution was, as you know, the result.

The old system, which had taken root from the outset in the government of the American Colonies, had long been preparing the way for a catastrophe. Each colony had a legislature of its own, responsible to the people, with complete control of legislation and supply. The governor was the replica of the King and responsible to the King, and he was the executive. If you read Parkman's account in his "History of the Seven Years' War" of the difficulties of the governor of Pennsylvania in obtaining from the Quaker assembly the money and laws necessary to enable him to protect the settlers on the frontier from massacre at the hand of the Indians and French, you will get an idea of the difficulties to which the situation gave rise. The difficulty of harmonizing the executive and legislature is one more familiar to you than to me. The whole lesson of Parkman's story is that the legislature and its electorate could not be expected to learn under that system the consequences of what they did, and, still more, the consequences of what they left undone. We are apt to think of responsible government as a system which makes those who rule responsible to those who obey, but the relation of responsibility is really bilateral. It is just as important that those who obey should recognize their responsibilities as those who rule. A real system of responsible government is one calculated to bring home as quickly as possible to a legislature and their electorate the consequences of their own acts. Thus, and thus only, will they draw wisdom from the lessons of experience.

The system was one which could not fail to throw the English executives on the one hand, and the

American legislatures and electorates on the other, into a posture of chronic antagonism. It was this antagonism which prepared the way for the American Revolution. After the Revolution, the States naturally elected their governors. This, as Lowell has pointed out, at least secured that the electorates and the governors could not remain in permanent antagonism to each other. It concentrates the final responsibility of the government in all its aspects on the electorate; but I understand that you still experience a good deal of difficulty from conflicts between the executive and legislature.

After the American Revolution, George III lost his reason, and the rise of Pitt to power reëstablished the system of responsible government as we now know it in England. But again, the British Government failed to appreciate or apply the lesson to those of the American colonies which remained under the British flag. The old system continued in Canada, if anything tightened, until in the thirties of the last century it produced rebellions in Ontario and Quebec. Lord Durham was sent out to report on the situation. In a report which remains one of the greatest documents in constitutional history, he demonstrated that any system of government must fail in which the executive is responsible to one authority and the legislature to another. For the first time he explained to the English people the meaning and importance of the innovation which they had achieved in their own system of responsible government. He persuaded them to apply that system to Canada, and in process of time it was also applied to Australia, New Zealand, and South Africa; to every

British country, in fact, in which the legislature was responsible to a genuine electorate. Lowell, in his work on the government of England—the counterpart of Bryce's "American Commonwealth"—reviews in masterly fashion the whole experience on this subject gained by the British Commonwealth since the time of Durham. He shows conclusively that wherever the dual system has been tried it has always failed. No less conclusively than Durham, he shows that it always must fail. British opinion has been singularly slow to learn from these eminent teachers or to read the lessons of its own experience. In Jamaica, Malta, and Rhodesia the old system was repeated, with the same evil results. The Transvaal was saved from it only by the election of 1906, followed by the decision of Campbell-Bannerman to suspend the Lyttelton Constitution and to grant full responsible government.

The question you will naturally ask is why the problem in India should not have been solved by granting the electorates full responsible government. The shortest answer I can give is that no genuine electorates existed as in Canada and all the other dominions, to which the government could be made responsible. An electorate is something more than a list of names. It is a body of citizens who can be trusted in the last resort to put the public interest before their own. If they fail to do so, one of two things must always happen. Either government ceases to be responsible to the electorate, or government ceases altogether. In Russia you have one result, in China the other. It is no use beating about the bush. It is not in human power to give a people responsible government except in so far as they are able to take it, and they can take it only in so far as an adequate number of citizens can be found to decide political issues, who know how to make those decisions with an eye to the public interests rather than their own. People in India are always talking as if responsible government were a matter of training politicians in efficiency. It is nothing of the kind; it is a question of training electorates. In communities where no such body of citizens has existed, it can be created only by giving limited responsibilities to the classes most likely to develop these qualities by exercise.

I have said that Morley allowed a certain number of members to be elected to the Indian legislatures. The timidity of his advisers in India reduced the electorates to a farce. British India, excluding the native states, is well over two hundred million souls. I found that on analysis there were only four thousand direct voters for the whole Legislative Council of India. One member was elected by a majority of nine votes. In the legislature of the United Provinces, with its population of forty-eight millions, there were only about three thousand people entitled to vote. The problem was to make electorates in the provinces as well as in India adequate in size and quality for the burden to be laid on them. The contention of some of us was that this would never be accomplished by giving vast oriental electorates power to control government with no responsibility for results. Let me take a case in point. "Universal free education" was one of the most popular cries in India. The real difficulty is the poverty of the country arising from the low productive capacity of the people. Under the Congress-League system, the legislatures could have ordered the immediate institution of universal education without having any responsibility for voting the money and imposing the taxes necessary to raise it. I remember that when it was proposed that the Indian electorate should be given the control of education, coupled with the responsibility for raising the taxes necessary to defray the cost, a nationalist paper in Bengal strenuously objected on the ground that such a position would make the Indian ministers unpopular. We are apt to think of political leaders as men in search of popularity. The truth is that, in any country able to govern itself, they are people who have learned to face the ordeal of doing unpopular things. That is why they are so anxious for all the popularity they can get. A country able to govern itself is one in which not only the politicians but the electorate have learned to endure things they dislike in the present in order to obtain objects they need in the future; and this faculty they acquire from the lessons which experience alone teaches: that future evils can be avoided only at the cost of present sacrifice.

The suggestion was that the electorates and legislatures might learn those qualities from experience if they were given responsibilities which, though limited, were real. To begin with, this suggestion was advanced in the following form: It was proposed that elective legislatures should be created in each province, with the ministers responsible to the legislatures, that is to say, removable by their votes. To these ministers the administration of education, local government, and roads and bridges was to be entrusted. The other duties of the government, especially those of maintaining order and administering justice, were to be left in the hands of the existing executive councils, responsible to the Secretary of State. In respect of all these reserved functions, the elected legislatures were to have advisory powers only.

This was the principle known as diarchy (which, as you see, is composed of two Greek words, δυο and ἀρχή—two rules). It is one capable of application in any number of ways. The above proposal was framed before I visited India, but after I had been there for a year, I began to feel that the vast provinces, which were in fact the satrapies of the old Mogul Empire, were far too large to be used as a basis for the institution of popular government. The United Provinces, as I have said, contains more people than the whole British Isles. Aptitude for responsible government has always been developed in much smaller communities than this. It was so in the United States, and I noticed that New York, the largest of its communities, contains only about ten million people. America, in fact, with its forty-eight states, seemed to me the model to which India should naturally look. I therefore suggested that the United Provinces should be cut up into four states, each containing about twelve million persons, and that all the other provinces should be divided into states on similar lines. You must realize that in India there are upwards of one hundred different languages. Throughout India English is used as the language of government, much in the same way as Latin was used by Europe in the Middle Ages. This *lingua anglicana* is one of the greatest boons which

England has conferred on India. It provides a common language in which the affairs of India can be discussed in an Indian legislature. But the use of a foreign language in politics is a serious impediment to the growth of popular government. Personally I thought that the people of India would learn what popular government means far more quickly in so far as they could discuss public affairs in their own tongues. I proposed, therefore, that the new states should be based, so far as possible, on linguistic areas. The province of Madras, for instance, includes four perfectly distinct linguistic areas, which might for convenience be divided into four states for the purpose of acquiring responsible government. The proposal was that each of these smaller states should have an electorate, a legislature, and a responsible minister of its own, and that education, local government, and roads and bridges should be entrusted at once to these ministers with correlative powers of legislation and taxation. The governments of the United Provinces and Madras would then continue to administer the other reserved powers as at present. It was further proposed that as the popular governments in the smaller states proved their fitness for responsible government, other powers should be transferred. Thus after a time the control of forests, of irrigation, and of liquor would be handed over one by one, until last of all the control of justice, police, and of all the provincial revenues should be transferred from the large province to the smaller states. The old provincial government would then vanish altogether, leaving the several states into which it had been divided in control of all provincial powers and responsible to state legislatures and electorates. By this process the nine great satrapies would eventually vanish, leaving some thirty self-governing states comparable to those of the United States. This would also have made it easier in future to bring the native states into the system of a federalized India. The largest of these native states is Hyderabad, which contains about thirteen millions. When this stage was accomplished, the time would then have arrived for making the government of India, which has charge of the defense, foreign affairs, railways, customs, and such like, responsible to an Indian electorate at large.

For historical reasons this proposal met with violent opposition. A few years before, an attempt had been made to partition the overgrown province of Bengal. The methods adopted were by no means happy. The partition of Bengal, which was on its merits undoubtedly a sound measure, was forced through in the teeth of opposition so violent that it was eventually reversed, though partition on different lines had to be effected. A country which does not govern itself becomes the prey of suspicion. The proposal to divide the great provinces into small states for the purpose of self-government was seen in India through the medium of all the passions aroused by the partition of Bengal. Personally I think that in this case the Government would have been wise to insist on the smaller areas; but the Government thought otherwise and decided to apply the principle of diarchy without dividing the great satrapies. The plan put into operation by the Government of India Bill of 1919 was in main outline that proposed before I visited India. In principle, two governments were instituted side by side in the same vast areas: one consisting of Indian ministers responsible to the legislature for the powers transferred to them; the other consisting of the executive council responsible for all the reserved powers to the British Parliament through the Secretary of State. The principle of keeping the two responsibilities distinct was blurred in the details. Indian ministers and the executive councillors were encouraged to think and act as one government. To me it has always seemed a positive danger that Indian ministers should be taught to lean on their British colleagues. They would, I venture to think, have been far more ready to learn the habit of taking responsibility were they placed in a position where they clearly have to rely on themselves, and this would have happened if they had stood alone in the smaller states. In an illuminating article in the *Atlantic Monthly,** which I hope you will all read if you have not read it, Mr. Van Tyne says: "Diarchy is in fact become in most cases a unitary government in which a governor sits in council with all his ministers, those responsible for the 'transferred' subjects, as well as those concerned with the 'reserved.'" It would be far better, in my opinion, if ministers felt they had to decide the questions transferred to them on their own exclusive responsibility.

Anything, however, was better than the establishment of irresponsible legislatures and electorates, towards which British and Indian opinion alike were drifting in 1917. No one can say as yet whether diarchy will prove the solution of a problem which affects

* July, 1922.

communities even greater than India. This much at any rate is certain, that the ultimate answer to the problem will be found not by endless debate but by trial alone. Proposals must be tried to see where they fail, and the failures corrected in the light of practical results. It is this which the experiment started in 1919 enables us to do. The principle of the commonwealth is, in truth, like the Kingdom of Heaven, to be found only where conscience is guided by the lamp of human experience. Aramaic, the language in which our Lord thought and spoke, has only one word for a state, which Greek translators who had not sounded the uttermost depths of his meaning rendered as "kingdom." Had Greek been his native tongue I think he would have spoken of the "commonwealth" of Heaven. The bearing of all this on our ultimate theme I shall try to develop in my next lecture.

LECTURE III

A Criterion of Values in International Affairs

In my previous lectures I did my best to present two national problems of which I happened to know something at first hand. I shall now try to state certain more general conclusions on the international problem to which these experiences have brought me. As these conclusions have to be compressed into one lecture I may seem to be more dogmatic than I really am. I take that risk and ask you to discount it.

Civilization is society organized in states. In our studies here we are treating the relations of states, and as the world is now practically organized into states, they cover the whole of human society. States, as distinguished from nations, are composed of the people inhabiting definite areas of the earth's surface who are all expected to obey one common direction.

The first question to be considered may be stated in various ways.

How is it that masses of men, usually amounting to millions, can be brought to obey a common direction?

By what authority is that direction exercised?

What is the sentiment which unites such a number

of persons in obedience to a common authority? Is self-interest, as commonly assumed, the ultimate motive of this obedience?

This assumption is contrary to evident facts, because individuals are willing to face even torture and death in obedience to the state. It is only in so far as citizens are willing to sacrifice themselves that states can exist. Self-interest may afford a motive for common action at a given moment. But it cannot supply a basis for continuous coöperation, because the interests of individuals are constantly shifting. Compact is no more the basis of the state than settlements of property are the bases of marriage. The ultimate bond is sacramental, or, to use the words of President Lincoln, is of the nature of dedication.

In the last analysis states are united not by self-interest but by moral ideas. Their foundations are laid in the spirit of man, not in his flesh.

This conclusion confronts us with a further question.

From what source is the guidance which a state gives to its members derived, or thought to be derived? I will illustrate my meaning. The Moslem believes that the laws he is called upon to obey were communicated to Mahomet by God. The ancient Israelite believed that King David's commands were divinely inspired. On the other hand, you and I do not believe that the Acts of Congress or Parliament, or the policies of Mr. Lloyd George or President Harding, are divinely inspired. But the process by which they are formulated is of vital importance to this inquiry.

To those who have studied the East the idea by which states in their primitive form are united is clear enough. The ruler is a person clothed with divine authority. The motive which induces obedience to his dictates is essentially religious. The ruler of an eastern state is either God, like the Lama of Thibet, or the spokesman of God, like Mahomet. Actual power to enforce obedience is accepted as evidence of divine authority, and may override the limits of national sentiment. When the present king of England visited India as its emperor he was treated by vast multitudes with a veneration which showed that they regarded his authority as divine. I have seen a letter to the government from a powerful notable in India at the time of the reforms, in which he said: "I do not understand the meaning of these proposals to transfer the king's authority to a public assembly. I have always obeyed His Majesty because I believed that he was the representative of God. I wish to be told where I am."

To men in this state of society, the orders of government are not regarded as the product of human intelligence, but are held to be inspired by divine wisdom. Hence the familiar saying in the Old Testament: "Rebellion is as the sin of witchcraft," the product of obedience to Satan instead of to God.

Until little more than two thousand years ago the whole of civilized society was possessed by these ideas. They still prevail with a vast majority in the east, and are to some extent the key to Mahatma Gandhi's immense influence in India. Up to our time they have continued to exercise a vast influence in Europe.

Their effect on the masses who entertain them, and on their institutions, cannot be ignored.

Monarchy is the product of these ideas. It is natural to suppose that God would communicate His wisdom to a single mind, and announce His commands through the lips of one, and not through the findings of a public assembly.

But the king cannot count on universal obedience, because there are impious people. He must therefore have an army to enforce obedience. The success of that army in extending the king's authority is evidence of his divine mission. Autocracy thus naturally leads to conquest.

As Bryce pointed out to you last year, the consequences of this view were less serious while the world believed in a multitude of gods, and each nation felt that its obedience was due to separate gods of its own. If there is room in heaven for a number of deities, so there is room on earth for a multitude of states obeying their various commands. But when men began to conceive God as one, the political results were terrific. Christendom was in mortal conflict with Islam. To the pious Moslem there were and still are no logical limits to the duty of conquest.

The effects of this idea on the individual are of even greater importance. In a state where the bond of union is simply the common duty of obedience to God there is little to exercise and develop men's sense of duty to each other. And where public policy and law are regarded as the product of Divine inspiration, the individual is not to be expected to examine their wisdom. Their own mutual relations are not a subject on which men are asked to reflect. Laws, like those of Moses or Manu, are regarded as divine. Scriptures, like the Vedas or Koran, are treated as the only source of recorded wisdom. When implored by the scholars of Alexandria to spare their library, the Mohammedan conqueror replied that either their books agreed with the Koran or else they did not. In the first case, they were unnecessary; in the second, they were impious and untrue. The greatest bridge which ever existed between ancient and modern civilization was given to the flames.

Oppressed by the weight of these ideas, men's characters and minds develop slowly. Growth is arrested and social conditions become static. Hence the fact that Asia, the home of civilization, is also a place where civilization has scarcely advanced for thousands of years, and has now begun to move only in response to the impulse received from Europe.

In the words of Bryce, the ideas which inspire autocracy are an illusion. Rather, let us say they are half-truths. In so far as they have taught the great majority of mankind the habit of obedience to a common authority, the debt we owe them is not to be ignored. They are broken lights by which men grope their way to a certain point and no farther. They cannot advance beyond autocracy until they learn to interpret their duty to God in terms of their duty to their neighbor. That is, in truth, the transition from the old dispensation to the new, from the law delivered in the thunders of Horeb to the sermon preached on a hilltop in Galilee.

The real bond which unites society is not terror of

God but the duty which men owe to each other. In the long run, society will grow more stable only in so far as this sense of mutual devotion is developed by exercise. Men love each other in so far as they are conscious of serving each other. The real sources of wisdom are not miraculous revelations; nor is ultimate truth embodied in Scripture. The elements of truth expressed in sacred laws and writings were the fruits of human experience. The only genuine oracles are those revealed to human intelligence guided by conscience. The facts of life are the only Scripture in which the eternal truths are written. A political system is sound in so far as it operates to keep men in touch with the facts of life, to practice them in reading their meaning, and to make them responsible for giving effect to the lesson. Nature is the only school in which discipline can teach the one cardinal virtue of self-control to men in the mass.

Such a system will germinate only in a soil where self-control, devotion to others, and clearness of mind are present to a certain degree. But once established it impregnates the soil with the spiritual foods drawn from the light and the air that nourish its roots. Its life fosters the virtues on which it depends. As the principle of autocracy tends to stagnation and decay, so that of the commonwealth tends to indefinite growth destined in time to embrace all human society. The least of all grains, it grows till its branches cover the whole earth, and the fowls of the air lodge therein.

The seeds of this principle first made their appearance in Greece, and the literature of Athens enables us to examine its earliest growth under a microscope. It shows to us a miniature commonwealth containing some few thousand citizens united by a sense of loyalty to each other. The strength of that mutual devotion is expressed for all time in the speech which Pericles delivered at the funeral of some of its citizens who had given their lives for the city, a speech destined to find its echo in the words uttered by Lincoln on the field of Gettysburg. In both these speeches we are conscious of a system in which men rejoice to live and die for each other.

The final authority to which the Athenians bowed was public opinion as expressed in laws framed by themselves in open discussion. Their word for obedience was *πειθόμενος*—being persuaded. But you have only to turn the pages of Plato and Aristotle to see that the law was regarded with a reverence never accorded to the decrees of a monarch. Socrates claimed no rights from the state, but saw no limits to the duty he owed to the state. He once refused to obey its commands, but only when he thought they were fatal to the state itself. In his philosophy there might be a duty of rebellion but never a right. He died a rebel, but his death was an act of devotion to his fellow citizens, as Christ's was an act of devotion to all mankind. A man must face death if he feels it his duty to break the law. The words: "Though freedom slay me I will trust in her" might well have been written on his grave. He recognized that as men are wanting in public spirit and as there is a point beyond which the most unselfish of men cannot be persuaded, so the law must, in the last instance, be enforced. The saying that force settles nothing is in open conflict with facts. No state can dispense with force until every citizen is all-knowing and wholly unselfish. The wisest thing ever uttered on the subject was written by your own Admiral Mahan: "The province of force in human affairs is to give moral ideas time to take root."

This tremendous respect for the laws, however, was based on reason and not on superstition. If any one thought them bad he was free to say so and give his reason. They could always be changed by persuading public opinion. The appeal to experience as interpreted by reason was open. The state was themselves. Its decisions were their own. For the consequences they had only themselves to thank or to blame. They reaped as they sowed. Their system was one which kept them in intimate contact with the facts of life. They were disciplined by nature to self-control.

Thus in Athens was developed a system in which the relations of men to each other are determined by laws framed in accordance with the experience of those who obey them. Its distinguishing mark is the rule of law. It accepts no limit to the loyalty claimed from its members. And in that loyalty is included the obligation not only to obey the law but also to enforce it. The use of force in a commonwealth is the necessary consequence of the claim which it makes on its citizens. And this claim is from its nature unique. The commonwealth cannot allow in its citizens an equal devotion to any other kind of organization. This claim to a loyalty overriding all others is sovereignty, and on occasion is exercised to the full. You and I belong to commonwealths which a few years ago claimed and exercised the right to send millions of citizens without question to face torture and death.

The justification of these principles is that they do in fact promote the development of human character and mind. They move society from stagnation to growth. They tend, in a word, to the making of men.

How came it that the Greek communities which first conceived these principles of society, and also applied them to the facts of political life, themselves so quickly perished? The answer to this question must be sought in the limits imposed on their application. The citizens of Athens were limited to the largest possible number of citizens who could listen to the voice of a single speaker. The only relations which could thus be brought within the realm of law were those which affected the people of one small city. Methods whereby the relations of that city to all the other cities of Greece could be brought within the rule of law, and included in one national commonwealth, were never conceived by the Greeks, or at any rate were conceived too late by Aratus. To adopt the admirable phrase which Bryce used in this place of the great nations of the world today, the cities of Greece remained in a state of nature to each other. The devotion which they felt for each other as Greeks went unexercised and unbreathed, and never became the bond of a national commonwealth. And so freedom perished in Greece, and fifteen centuries had to pass before the principle of the commonwealth could be realized in terms of a national state.

Rome survived by exchanging the principle of the

commonwealth for that of autocracy. It is, as I have said, in accordance with the nature of despotisms to embrace any number of subjects. The Roman Empire was expanded to include the whole of the countries surrounding the Mediterranean. The Greek commonwealths were smothered in the process.

It was by the expedient of representation that England succeeded where the Greeks had failed. The principle of basing government on the experience of the governed was thus applied to a country far too large for its people ever to assemble in one place. Protected by the seas there emerged a commonwealth strong enough to resist the great autocracies of Europe. By the enterprise of its merchants and the prowess of its sailors, above all by the devotion of some of its children to the essential principles of the parent community, a nation organized on those principles was firmly established in America. But those two nations were not destined to solve the problem which had baffled the genius of the Greeks. The principle of representation could not of itself avail to unite under one rule of law two nations divided by three thousand miles of sea. They fell apart, and today stand to each other in a state of nature.

It must, however, be held in mind that the eastern shore of the United States is separated from its western shore by a distance approximately equal to that which divides Cornwall from Maine. The people of California and those of New England could not have been united in one commonwealth merely by virtue of representation in a common assembly, if only for the reason that one government would never have been able to discharge all the business necessary for the number of people destined to occupy so vast an area. The problem was solved by a device no less momentous in the history of freedom than that of representation. It was the device of leaving to provincial communities, which for historical reasons are misdescribed as states, every possible function of government which those communities can discharge for themselves. It is only in matters too great for those communities to handle that the assembly of the nation at large is asked to control.

I speak of America as a nation, but if you will turn back to the writings of one hundred and forty years ago you will find that your forefathers constantly referred to the thirteen parent states as "these nations." You would never think of calling Massachusetts a nation today. But a million lives were sacrificed in order to establish the principle that the United States was the commonwealth to which the ultimate loyalty of its citizens was due. The possibility of a commonwealth embracing any number of people included in one territory, however large, was demonstrated thereby. The principles which have enabled Canada, Germany, the Argentine, Australia, and South Africa to apply self-government to their vast areas were first reduced to practice at Philadelphia. It is that model which inspires countries like India and China with hope. But Gettysburg was needed to assert those principles. If you think of the results achieved by your own civil war, you will see what Mahan meant when he said that "the province of force in human affairs is to give moral ideas time to take root."

To Greeks so fearless in mind as Plato and Aristotle a commonwealth larger than a single city was inconceivable. They were unable to foresee the two great political inventions of the Anglo-Saxon race, representation and federation. I point to this warning, because today practical statesmen assume, and act upon the assumption, that commonwealths on the scale of the United States are the largest units of mankind to which the rule of law properly so-called can ever be applied. That nations on this scale are for ever to remain in a state of nature to each other, that the widest and most important of human relations are always to remain in the realm of anarchy, is accepted as an axiom by rational minds. The vision of a world commonwealth may serve as the theme of a peroration; but a public man suspected of using that ideal as the practical criterion of policy in international affairs is in real danger. I am not referring to those whose outlook is purely national. To them a policy is right or wrong only in so far as it tends to the material loss or gain of their country. But to those who have risen to a point of view which deserves to be called international the test usually applied to policies is simply whether they make for peace or war. Now for nations to accept peace as the criterion of policy is exactly as though men were to seek physical health as the criterion of conduct. People whose lives are regulated mainly by physical health become hypochondriacs, and miss the very object they seek. "He that seeks to save his life shall lose it." Among people whose conduct is guided by the aim to live rightly the general level of physical health will be far higher.

And so with states. To them peace is as physical health to the individual. But health is only one element and by no means the chief one, in well-being, which is best described in the trite phrase *mens sana in corpore sano*—a sound body regulated by a well ordered mind. The right system of society is one composed of such men, and therefore one calculated to reproduce them in a higher degree and in greater numbers.

As health is worth risking for right living, so is health a product of right living. And as peace is worth risking for freedom, so peace is a product of freedom. "He that seeks to lose his life shall save it." The principle I have to submit for your serious consideration is that the test by which all policies should be proved is not whether they help to avert an immediate outbreak of war, but whether they tend to advance freedom among men.

It is from this point of view that I ask you to consider the union which in this continent embraces your forty-eight states. The authors of the "Federalist" saw clearly enough that unless the union were effected, the separate states would inevitably drift into internecine war. But avoidance of war was not the motive which mainly actuated the fathers of your Constitution. The object to which they looked was national self-control, the verities of responsible government. In achieving that object they actually made the greatest contribution to the peace of the world which had ever been accomplished. I ask you to consider what the effect on the international situation would be, if in America today there were forty-eight separate republics, each with a foreign department, an army, and a general staff of its own. Do you blame us if we draw our own conclusions from the lesson taught by yourselves?

I have dared to suggest that the growth of freedom will not be complete even when groups so large as those contained in India, China, or Central Africa have, like the United States, each been rendered amenable to law made by themselves. The view to which South Africa and India have led me is that all policies in the last analysis now turn on the mutual relations of the white races of Europe, America, and Australia to those of Asia and Africa. If this view is right, then there can be no final achievement in human affairs until these relations are made subject to law controlled by all the people concerned, in so far as they are fit to exercise such control. And before you set this view down as an idle dream, I ask you to reflect that I belong to an international state in which vast sections of all these continents have in fact been brought within the jurisdiction of the rule of law. It is true that that law is in law amenable only to the will of the British people. It is not amenable even to the peoples of Canada, Australasia, and South Africa. And by reason of this glaring defect this vast international state, including one out of every four living men, has rightly been called an empire. It is just because some of us believe that this international state must perish unless it labors to cure this defect that we have sought to change its name from empire to commonwealth.

If the time is not yet ripe to give Indians a share in making the laws which determine their relations to the rest of the world, it is merely because they have not as yet achieved control of their own relations to each other. I say this without imputing the slightest blame to Indians themselves. Their ancestors attained a civilization long before ours had emerged from barbarism, and I have tried to explain why they in common with the rest of Asia have allowed us to outstrip their political development. Under British rule they have made a notable advance in the arts of life, in learning and in physical equipment. And if a similar advance has not been made toward self-government, the fault has been ours rather than theirs. Like South Africa, India is a microcosm, though on an immensely large scale, for it contains upwards of 300,000,000 human beings, a sixth part of the whole human race. It is a continent rather than a country, including a welter of religions and languages, castes, tribes, and races at all the stages of barbarism and civilization. The enforcement of law and the establishment of order was the first condition of future progress, and it was this inestimable boon which British rulers have given to India. The mistake has been in continuing to concentrate on the maintenance of order as if order were an end in itself. Measures to create the foundations of order in the character of Indians themselves involved the taking of risks, and we did not take those risks in time. We ignored the fact that responsibility is the only sure foundation for law. To live, freedom must live dangerously.

The foundations of responsible government in India ought to have been laid years ago in local government. Lord Ripon essayed the task in 1880. In districts and municipalities representative councils were instituted, but their educational effect was largely sterilized by the British officials entrusted with their organization; though not from any unworthy motive. So high was their own standard of honor and efficiency that the officers could not bear to see the public interest suffer at the hands of the Indian councils. With tireless energy they guided their proceedings, and so succeeded that the British officers in fact became the mainsprings of the local administrations. Protected from the worst consequences of their own indolence and mistakes, the local electorates learned little or nothing. But meanwhile the schools and colleges were at work, and the educated classes were gradually losing the primitive beliefs upon which government in the East has rested. They were ceasing to believe that the power of rulers to rule is evidence of the divine authority, and with that belief the power to rule inevitably crumbles. In seeking to maintain order, and that alone, we have not considered enough whether the foundations would sustain the ever-increasing burden of the structure raised on them. Here again "he that seeks to save his life shall lose it." To neglect freedom and pursue peace as the aim of human endeavor is to end by destroying both; for anarchy is the negation not only of law but also of liberty. The true lesson to be learned from Russia is less the folly of neglecting order than the unwisdom of failing to found it on responsibility. To study India as a microcosm is also to understand the peril of treating peace as the test of policy in international affairs.

Do not understand me, however, as depreciating the work which England has accomplished for India. It is just because I believe so intensely in that work that I dwell on the mistakes. The most perilous task which a commonwealth can undertake is to attempt to govern other races. It cannot be done without the gravest risk to the principles upon which its own institutions are based. Athens and Rome are both warnings on that point. I am infinitely proud that my own countrymen did not shrink from the perils involved. In order to grow, freedom must live dangerously. Right principles of action will be discovered only by those with the daring to act. In the last analysis, men learn only by making mistakes, and dwelling on them; for mistakes can be remedied if recognized in time, and I think that we have recognized our mistakes in India in time. Frankly, I believe that the cause of freedom in the East has gained immeasurably by the inclusion of India in a commonwealth which centers in the West. I believe that, so, India will travel faster and more easily toward the verities of responsible government than countries left in the position of Persia or China.

Throughout these lectures I have spoken of the principle of the commonwealth and of responsible government. I have dwelt on the need and the duty of men to govern themselves, and not on their right to do so. The term "democracy" has scarcely crossed my lips, if at all. The principle of the commonwealth and that of democracy are two distinct though closely connected ideas. A commonwealth presupposes a certain capacity in a certain number of its citizens to govern themselves. It is a polity founded on the will of those who are in some sort capable of political judgment; that is to say, of the citizens who are able to put public interests before their own. The English polity in the time of Cromwell was, I think, entitled to the name of commonwealth, though the voters in whom political decisions were vested were the merest fraction of the whole population. Universal suffrage has never existed and never will. Infants and criminals and aliens are always excluded from the franchise, infants because they have yet to learn to put the public interest before their own, criminals because they have proved their incapacity to do so, and aliens because, although they may live in the country and are amenable to its laws, their loyalty is due to another community. In the most advanced democracies, like those of New Zealand, the voters include scarcely more than half the population.

In the view of Plato and Aristotle the idea of a commonwealth was an aristocracy, a system in which the franchise was invested in the ἄριστοι, in the best of the citizens, or in other words, in those who are fit for political power. To them democracy implied a premature extension of the franchise to citizens not yet ready for the burden, and they abhorred it as such. They viewed democracy as a step toward anarchy, not leading back to a monarchy based on divine right, but to tyranny based on no principle whatever but that of organized force. The first French empire and the recent history of Russia and China illustrate the process.

Plato was always in search of an ἰδέα τοῦ ἀγαθοῦ, an idea of the good, an ultimate goal toward which the commonwealth looks. Scholars dispute how he conceived this goal. What matters to us is not how Plato conceived the goal of freedom, but what it is. To you I hazard the suggestion that the end and object of all policy should be to make more men more fit for the exercise of political responsibility. The commonwealth is not an end in itself, but exists only to propagate freedom in the souls of men, which, rightly understood, is a sense of responsibility in themselves for others. In so far as it succeeds in this object the commonwealth will flourish, but its visible success is to be valued only as a sign that its function in promoting the growth of human souls is in active process. A commonwealth which is not progressing toward democracy is in danger of losing sight of its ultimate goal.

There is, however, another principle of psychology which the Greeks could scarcely discern as we do now. It is the elementary principle that human faculties will grow only by exercise. In India I was constantly told that it was idle to think of beginning responsible government until a large body of the people were educated. My answer to this argument is that it involves a misconception of education, and of the object which education seeks to attain. In schools and colleges you can teach knowledge, but not wisdom, which is the end of education rightly conceived. Wisdom imports something more than knowledge. It involves the power not only to see the course which is right, but also to follow it when it runs counter to our own interests. And this wisdom comes only from contact with facts. Wisdom is taught only by nature herself in the school of responsibility. Professors will never create electorates fit for political decisions. That fitness will not begin to develop until men are called upon not only to decide public questions but also to experience the consequences of their own decisions. Men must be given scope to hurt themselves without destroying themselves. The problem you have to face in the Philippines and we have to face in India, is how much scope you can give the people to hurt themselves without destroying the fabric of government altogether.

The danger and difficulty are always greatest at the outset, and both diminish if the start succeeds. In a state where a large body has already proved its fitness for responsible government it is easy and safe to extend the franchise. In the Cape Colony, for instance, where one-fourth of the population was European, it was comparatively safe to extend the franchise to the natives. In Natal, where only one-eleventh was European, the first step to a native franchise is incredibly difficult.

You cannot establish responsible government if in the process you destroy government, because government is the only foundation of responsible government.

It is, however, the most dangerous fallacy to suppose that the principle of the commonwealth, or in other words freedom, depends only on giving the vote to more people. The whole upshot of what I had to say about South Africa was that the verities of responsible self-government may be destroyed if the interests common to a whole community are parceled out between two or more electorates. And exactly the reverse may happen in a great community if it fails to devolve the control of local interests on local authorities, simply for the reason that there are not enough hours in the day or days in the year for the central government to meet the multifarious needs of the people. It is exactly this evil from which the British Isles are suffering today. In America the verities of responsible government would perish if you destroyed the forty-eight state governments and transferred their functions to Washington. They would perish no less if you destroyed the federal government on the assumption that its functions could be left to the forty-eight states. I have urged that all policies and political systems should be judged by their fitness to advance responsible government. But the test is far from easy to apply, and certainly does not consist merely in gauging the proportion of voters. From the path to freedom there are many byways which lead only to the castles of despair. There is many an arbor tempting the pilgrim to enchanted sleep. His one security is to glance now and again where the glow in the sky marks the place of the golden city. "The price of freedom is eternal vigilance." Here surely for one short hour we may lift our eyes to the far horizon.

The relations of the peoples of Europe and America to those of Asia and Africa is, I have submitted, the ultimate problem of politics. The real question is how to bring those relations within the realm of law properly so called. The solution of that problem involves the creation of a commonwealth large enough to include not merely cities, districts, or provinces, but whole nations, each with a national government of its own. And before you reject this conclusion as the dream of a visionary, I ask you to reflect that nations together equal to a fourth of mankind have already been brought within the scope of one paramount law. The international state miscalled the British Empire is a genuine commonwealth of nations in the making. The democracies of Great Britain, of Ireland, of Canada, Australasia, and South Africa, that immense section of Asia contained in India, vast areas of Central Africa whose peoples are slowly emerging from savagery, together with a large number of islands scattered over all the seas and continents, are no longer in a state of nature to each other. They are in fact governed by law, a law which in practice does maintain between them a peace such as could not exist under any other condition. But that is not all. This vast congeries of nations in matters of peace and war stands to all other nations outside their circle as one international state. They are all at peace or at war together. Germany ignored this fact to her ruin. She never foresaw that forces from Canada, India, Australasia, and South Africa would throw themselves into the struggle. Yet without these forces the line could not have been held till America entered to turn the scale. Have you ever thought what this international commonwealth means to the peace of the world?

China, the only other state comparable in size, is a wing of the human edifice. Its destruction might shake but would scarcely destroy the whole fabric of society. But this commonwealth of nations is a steel frame spread through the whole structure, and were it to collapse the peace of the world would fall in unspeakable ruin. The five continents are poised on its arches. But I weigh my words when I say that unless the principle of the commonwealth steadily replaces the principle of empire in its structure, those arches will collapse. The development of this commonwealth on the principles which inspire it, and a right understanding of what those principles mean, is of vital importance to the whole world.

It has always seemed to me strange that cosmopolitans who dream of a world government and a parliament of man go out of their way to condemn any institution which is in fact a practical step toward their ideal. They are blind to actual achievements, and have eyes only for their failures and defects. If we had but vision, the figure of our dreams is about us in the making. Its substance is here to be handled and seen.

> The angels keep their ancient places;
> Turn but a stone, and start a wing!
> 'Tis we, 'tis our estrangèd faces
> That miss the many-splendored thing.

The incorporation of great sections of Asia and Africa in one world commonwealth affords the best conditions under which those races can attain to the verities of responsible government; provided always that those in whom political power already vests continue to realize that the growth of responsible government, and not peace, is the ultimate goal in view. The basic problem of the world, that of bringing the peoples of Europe, Asia, and Africa into some stable relation with each other, is destined, I believe, to be solved only in terms of the state inspired by the principles of the commonwealth. We are fatally inclined to think of liberty as something opposed to the rule of law, and to see in the state the negation of freedom. The rule of law is coincident with the state, and men achieve freedom only in so far as more communities can be gathered in the circle of a single polity.

A time has arrived when a further extension of freedom depends on our power of solving the problem —how to include in one commonwealth, without destroying its character as such, whole nations in varying stages of progress. The essence of freedom is self-discipline. Her austere aspect is the state, and through all the ages men have fled her approach, in their blindness avoiding the refuge they desire. Some of you may have read a religious poem called "The Hound of Heaven," in which the poet tells how he sought to escape his Divine pursuer:

> I fled Him, down the nights and down the days;
> I fled Him, down the arches of the years;
> I fled Him, down the labyrinthine ways
> Of my own mind; and in the mist of tears
> I hid from Him, and under running laughter.
> Up vistaed hopes I sped;
> And shot precipitated
> Adown Titanic glooms of chasmèd fears,
> From those strong Feet that followed, followed after.

So, outlaw-wise, man seeks for refuge in pleasure, in nature, in knowledge, till at last he falls and is overwhelmed by "this tremendous lover."

> Halts by me that footfall:
> Is my gloom, after all,
> Shade of His hand, outstretched caressingly?

"Ah, fondest, blindest, weakest,
I am He Whom thou seekest!
Thou dravest love from thee, who dravest Me."

Religion and politics are but two aspects of life; to ignore one is to miss the meaning of the other. The root principle of the commonwealth is love, and the sense of duty to each other which love inspires in men. And so it has moved down the ages, clothed in the stern attributes of the state, bursting the walls of cities, effacing the frontiers of nations, transcending the oceans and bridging their coasts. And so it will move until it has breached the barriers which divide the races of men and continents of the world, till freedom shall cover the whole earth as the waters cover the sea.

NOTE.—Data upon which the foregoing lectures are based will be found in the following publications: The Selborne memorandum, printed as a government blue-book; "The Government of South Africa" (two volumes, a few copies of which are still obtainable from the Oxford University Press); "The Problem of the Commonwealth" (Macmillan's); "The Commonwealth of Nations" (Macmillan's); and "Dyarchy" (Oxford University Press).

INDEX

THE PREVENTION OF WAR

INDEX

Action, need for, 16
Africa, governed by civilized people, 60
Akbar, 108
  government of, 109
  reform of, 111
Alexander II, and League of Peace, 11
All-India Moslem League, at Lucknow, 122
Alternative systems, failure to create, causes war, 14
American commonwealth, applicable to world problems, 65
  three fundamental ideas of, 64
Anarchy, menace of day, 8
Aristocracy, Greek idea of, 152
Aristotle, idea of commonwealth, 152
Army, instrument of divine authority in East, 138
Asiatic population, exceeds white in Natal, 100
  in South Africa, 100
Association of Nations, compared with Confederation, 1781-89, 54, 55
Autocracy, illusion, 139

Baba, 108
Balfour, on peace movements, 15
Bismarck and modern Germany, relation of, to world peace, 11
Boers, customs, 89
Botha, 106
Botha, and South African Union, 105
  and Jameson, 106
British, assent to South African Union, 105
  under Dutch generals in South Africa, 105
British and French in India, 110
British Commonwealth, a kind of world unity, 71
  and peace of the world, 156, 157
British East India Company, 108
  abolished, 116
  founded, 82
  seizes Cape Town, 82
  struggles with France, 82
British Empire, a commonwealth of nations, 156
British government, policy of, in South Africa, 83
British immigration in South Africa, 88
British intervention in native affairs of India, 114
British officials and responsible government in India, 150
British political system in India, 116
British purchase of diamond fields in South Africa, 87
British South African Company, 90
Bryce, Lord, 77, 78
  on responsibility in government, 127
Burke, Edmund, 112

Cadastral survey, 113
Campbell-Bannerman, 127
 and responsible government for Transvaal and Orange Free State, 102
Canada, government of, 126
Cape Colony, cultivated by Dutch East India Company, 80
 nature of population of, 80
Cape Town, 80
 inland spread of Dutch population, 81
 key to Eastern trade, 82
 port of call for East India Company, 80
 purchased by England, 82
 seized by British East India Company, 82
Centralization, due to risk of war, 68
Charlemagne, and universal peace, 61
China, no conscious interest in government, 60
Chinese labor, imported in South Africa, 101
 revulsion of feeling against, in England, 102
Christendom vs. Islam in India, 138
Clive, 110, 112
 and Indian reform, 113
 and Indian revenue, 113
Coast towns in India created by British, 109
Commission to study native question in South Africa, 101
Commonwealth, Greek idea of, 152
 and democracy, difference between, 151, 152
Commonwealth of nations, 155
Community law, only means of peace, 19
Community of nations, abolishes war between states, 37
Competition of armaments, 39
Confederation 1781-89, reasons for failure of, 55
Congress-League reforms in India, 122, 123
Constitutional machinery for settling disputes, lacking, 30, 49
 leads to peace, 26
 necessary to avoid war, 51
 not impossible, 72
Constitutionality, development of, in western United States, 30
Constructive thought, need of, for prevention of war, 13
Coöperation, international, 36
Corruption, and British politics, 112
Cosmopolitan state, undesirable, 59
Customs, a factor in South African Union, 100
Customs convention in South Africa, 97, 98
Customs dispute in South Africa, 85, 86

Dalhousie, Lord, 114, 118, 119
Democracy, as a preventive of war, 20
 and commonwealth, 151, 152
 Greek attitude toward, 152
Diamond discovery, land dispute between provinces in South Africa, 86
Diarchy, 130, 132, 133
 Van Tyne on, 133
Diplomacy, only alternative to war, 7
 not satisfactory for settling disputes, 27
Disarmament, a step toward peace, 52
 impossible without alternative, 53
 not a solution, 52
Dissimilarity of nations, a problem in world democratic organization, 59-61
Divine authority of ruler in East, 137
Dupleix, policy of, 110

Durham, Lord, and responsible government of Canada, 126, 127
Dutch East India Company incorporated, 79
Dutch merchants, and shipping of Eastern produce, 79
Duty to fellow man, bond of unity, 140
Duty to state, first recognized by Greeks, 141

East, granted to Portuguese by Papal Bull, 79
Economic chaos, menace of day, 8
Education, and Indian electorate, 128, 129
  in India, urged by British public opinion, 119
  of natives in Cape Colony, 101
  of natives in Transvaal and Orange Free State, 101
Electorate, and universal education in India, 128, 129
England and France, struggle between, in eighteenth century, 110
England, purchase of Cape Town by, 82
English, the common language of India, 130, 131
English in South Africa, history of, 82
Equal rights to all civilized men, 101
European population in South Africa, 100
Evangelical movement and slavery, 82
Extra-territorial sphere, mechanism for, 69

Fear, most effective preventive of war, 20
Federal democracy, not applicable to world as whole, 64
Federal system, supplants confederation, 55
Federalism, and responsible constitutional government, 63
  invented by America, 63
"Federalist," 70
Federation, in United States, 145, 146
Fiske, John, on future wars, 10
Force, Admiral Mahan on, 142
  in international relations, only court of appeal, 7
  must be supplanted by law, 50
  need for, 142
  only arbiter for communities, 30
Formal international organization, not essential, 37
France and England, struggle between, in eighteenth century, 110
France, and modern European democracy, 64
Free institutions, India in relation to development of, 110
Freedom, advancement of, test of all policies, 147
  proper aim of government, 150
  result of single polity, 158
French and British in India, 110
French trading company in India, 110
Future wars, late war no security against, 8

"General good," as a standard, 37
  disputes settled from viewpoint of, 37
  lack of interest in, cause of war, 34, 39
  only hope of Europe, 44
  only point of view for world, 45
  promotion of, standard of national conduct, 58
  recognition of, necessary for peace, 44
German ambitions in South Africa, 90, 91
Germany and universal empire, attempt at universal peace, 61

Gladstone, and Transvaal, 87
Glenelg orders return of land to natives, 83
Gold, discovery of, at Witwatersrand, 88
  discovery of, effect of, on transportation in Transvaal, 99, 100
Golden Rule, good business, 45
Government of Germany, responsible for militarism and world war, 39
Greek city state, failure of, 62
Greek commonwealth, based on public opinion, 141, 142
  failure of, 143
Grey, Sir George, and unity of South Africa, 84

Hague, The, 11
Holy Alliance, attempt at permanent peace, 11
  attitude of England toward, 11
  competitive armaments and, 11
  Crimean War and, 11
  revolutions of 1848 and, 11
Human progress, 47

Idealism, dangers of, 12, 13
India, advancement of, under British rule, 149
  and development of free institutions, 100
  government of, 117, 118
  not yet in control of own relations, 149
  sea route to, and settlement of South Africa, 78, 79
  under British, 114
  under native princes, 114
Indian conditions, parliamentary investigations of, 112
Indian government, theory of, 111
Indian ministers, reliance of, on British, 133
Indian National Congress, 120, 122
  demands of, 120
Individual concessions to social community, responsible for order, 31
Inequality of black and white in South Africa, 101
Inertia, obstacle to organization of democratic state, 62
Innocent III, and universal peace, 61
Intercourse between states, inevitable, 29, 30
International conference, Balfour on, 15
  cannot end war, 54
  essential to international understanding, 54
  inadequate, 14
International coöperation, 56
International court, judicial, not legislative, 53, 54
  not sufficient, 53
  step toward peace, 53
International world, compared with western United States, 19

Jameson, Dr., 91, 92
  advance of, on Johannesburg, 92
  and Botha, 106
  and South African Union, 105, 106
Japan and United States, friction between, removed by Washington conference, 22
Johannesburg, gold discovery, 88

Kaapstad, founded, 80
Kant, "On Perpetual Peace," 10
Kruger, 92

Languages of India, 130
Law and constitutional government vs. force, 17, 18
Law, distinguishing mark of Greek government, 142
  indispensable to peace, 50
  of humanity, necessity of, to prevent war, 37
  to supplant force, 50
  universality of, developed by Rome, 62

Laws, divine, in India, 139
League of independent nations, 55
Liberty, goal of human activity, 13
Linguistic areas, as a basis of political divisions in India, 131
Lloyd George, action of, on British shipping, 45
Lobengula, 90
Local government, in America, 145
  need of, 155
Lyttelton Constitution, 127

Macaulay, Lord, influence of, on education, 119
Machinery for adjusting international disputes, dependent upon large human community, 46
  lacking, 33
Mahan, Admiral, 110
  on force, 142
Mahatma Gandhi, 137
Majuba Hill, British defeat at, 87
Mayflower Compact, fundamental idea of civilized community, 31, 32
Mechanical cause of war, 36
Military autocracies, a cause of war, 21
Military time-table, 23
  will reappear, 25
Milner, Lord, 94
  and South African tariff, 96
  appoints commission on native question, 101
  policy of, 102
Minto, Lord, 120
Modern invention and world wars, 12
Mogul, meaning of, 108
Mogul emperor, last one dethroned, 116
Mogul empire, 108
  government of, 108, 109
  religion of, 108
Monarchy, divine, 138
Monroe Doctrine, 11
Montagu, on responsible government of India, 121, 122
Moral outlook, advance of, necessary for world organization, 69, 70
Morley, and Indian government, 120
Moslem idea of conquest, 138

Napoleon, and universal peace, 61
Napoleon's confederation of European peoples, 10
Natal, foundation of republic by Boers, 83
National interests, prevent settlement of present-day problems, 42, 43
National passion, attempts to curb, at Peace Conference, 40
National preoccupation, cause of failure to prevent war, 38
Native question, a cause of difference among colonies in South Africa, 102
National self-government, only foundation for world peace, 61, 62
National selfishness, psychological root of war, 36
  obstacle to larger human communities, 47
Nations, dissimilarity of, obstacle to world democratic organization, 59-61
Natural sciences, and war, 11, 12
Negro population in South Africa, 100
Netherlands and Spain at war, effect of on Indian trade, 79

Obligations of war, 36
Obstacles to world democratic organization, 59-61
Orange Free State, settlement of, by Boers, 83

Papacy, and universal peace, 61

Paris Peace Conference, decisions of, for "general good," 40
Parliamentary government, development of in England, 123, 124
Pastoralists, Dutch, in interior of South Africa, 81
attitude of, toward Dutch East India Company, 81
Patriotism, breeder of hatred, 36
geographical limits of, 35
higher than racialism and tribalism, 35
Peace, impossible with self-centered interests, 43
Peace Conference, unsuccessful, because of national point of view, 41
Penn, William, on government and peace, 51
Pepper, rise in price of foundation of British East India Company, 82
Permanent peace, attempts to establish, 11
Pilgrim Fathers, and first written constitution, 58
Plato, on commonwealth, 152
Political control of inferiors, obligations of, 36
Political mechanism, a constitutional means of settling disputes, 51
Political responsibility, 153
Political union of South Africa, a necessity, 95
Popular government in India, proposal for, 131, 132
Portuguese trade in Indies, 79
Pretoria Convention, 90
Principle of British Government in India, proclaimed by Victoria, 116
Proclamation of Queen Victoria, 121
Productive capacity, problem in India, 128, 129
Progress and war, 13
Progress of humanity, faith in, not in politics, 34
Progress of world, object of international policy, 58
"Project of a Treaty for Perpetual Peace," 11
Prussianism, effective operative cause of Great War, 23
Psychological root of war, national selfishness, 36
Public opinion, on India, 112
on South Africa, 104
on world war, today, 12
opposed to another war, 8

Race of armaments, 39
Railroads in India, 115
Railways, a factor in South African Union, 100
Rebellion of Beyers, 107
Religion and politics, two aspects of life, 159
Representation, and world democratic organization, 61
Representation in England, reason for successful government, 144
Representative government, invented by England, 63
Representative government in India, 120, 121
Resolutions against war, inadequate, 14
failure of, in the past, 15
Responsibility, necessity of, for peace, 150
Responsible government, a question of training electorates, 128
advancement of, criterion of political systems, 155
and local government, in India, 149
in America, 125
in India, recognized by England, 122
Revenue-collection, in India, 111
influence of, on British government in India, 113
Revenues, and East India Company, 112
in India, 113

Rhodes, Cecil, 88, 91
and Bechuanaland, 90
and Lobengula, 90
founds British South African Company, 90
prime minister of Cape Colony, 89
recognizes need of unity of South Africa, 90, 91
use of British government in South Africa, 90
Rhodesia, 106
Ripon, Lord, and principle of representation in local government, 120
and responsible government in India, 149
Roman autocracy, 144
Rome, and universal peace, 61
Rule of law, in British Empire, 148

St. Helena, half-way house of British East India Company, 82
St. Pierre, Abbé de, "A Project of a Treaty for Perpetual Peace," 10
Satraps, native, collapse of, 113
Seaman, Owen, quoted, 74
Sea power, 110
Secretary of State for India created, 116
Selborne, 94
and South African Union, policy of, 102
Self-government, a necessity and duty, 151
a necessity for South Africa, 91
essential to world democratic organization, lacking, 61
Separate sovereign states, cause of war, 16, 25, 36
Sepoy mutiny, 115
organized modern equipment cause of, 115
results of, 116
Seven Years' War, 110
Slavery in South Africa, abolished, 83
Smuts, and South African Union, 105
South Africa, key to empire in India, 83
no responsible government to settle disputes in, 86
systems of government in, 94
South African question, a conflict of states, 103
history of, 78, 79
not a conflict of British and Boers, 103
South African Union, and World War, 107
South African unity, a necessity, 85
South African War, causes of, 85
result of, 93
Sovereignty, 67
States, moral ideas basis of union of, 136
Sugar importation, in Natal, 98
effect of customs convention on, 98
Super-state, 65, 66

Tariff, in South African communities, 95
Transportation, improvement of, in India, under Dalhousie, 114, 115
Transvaal, annexed to British possessions, 87
Transvaal Republic reëstablished, 87

Uitlanders, 88
denied share in government, 88
Union of South Africa, 87
United Provinces, 117
United States, as a model for Indian government, 130
cause of failure to regulate world difficulties, 41
example of subordination to "general good," 44

United States, withdrawal of, from post-war counsels, blow to Europe, 41
United States and Japan, war between, averted by Washington conference, 22
Universal disarmament, not universal peace, 52, 53
Universal peace, attempts to establish, 61

Van Tyne, quoted, 131
Vote, accorded natives in Cape Colony, 101
  not accorded natives in Transvaal and Free State, 101

War, and nature, 13
  and progress, 13
  enemy of democracy, 68
Warehouses, established by British East India Company in India, 109
  fortification of, led to founding of large cities in India, 109
Wars of the past, results of, 9
Washington Conference, war between United States and Japan averted by, 22
Welfare of the whole, 49
Western United States, constitutional development of, 30
Wilberforce, and slavery agitation, 82
World, a single community, 58
World commonwealth, 146
  conducive to responsible government, 158
  progress toward democracy, 153
World constitution, basis of peace in democratic communities, 52
  curtailment of national sovereignty by, 66
  need of, to promote international justice, 52
  only substitute for war, 52
World organization, only real sovereignty, 67
World patriotism, preliminary to end war, 37
World peace, national self-government only foundation for, 61, 62
World point of view, return to, necessary, 43
World problems, political, not judicial, 54
World state like national state, impossible, 59, 60
World unity, United States as an example of, 68
World War, causes of, 9
  effect of, on India, 121
  forerunners of, 38
  inevitableness of, 37
Worship of nation, prevents growth of sentiment for humanity, 35